FUNNY
MUMMY

This edition published by Prion in 2009
an imprint of the Carlton Publishing Group
20 Mortimer Street
London W1T 3JW

ISBN 978-1-85375-709-9

Printed in the UK by CPI Mackays, Chatham, ME5 8TD

The contents of this book previously appeared in
Laugh With Mother

FUNNY MUMMY

Funny Stuff For Mums

Mike Haskins & Clive Whichelow

Introduction

It's not easy being a mum is it? If it were, dads would do it. In fact, if men had to go through nine months of pregnancy and then the joys of childbirth we would probably have a very much smaller population. We may not even have a population at all.

Anyway, this little volume isn't about man-bashing – what you do in your spare time is nothing to do with us. This book is a celebration of what it is to be a mum – the laughs, the tears, the joys and the ironing. Let's face it, if you didn't laugh at some of the things mums have to put up with, you'd probably be bawling your head off along with the baby.

But it's nice to know you're not alone. People have been having trouble with their kids ever since God told Adam and Eve to refrain from scrumping in the Garden of Eden. Did they listen? Of course not. In fact one of the surest ways to get your kids to do anything is to ban them from doing it.

And what about dads? They do their bit, bless them. You cook meals and prepare lunchboxes day in, day out all week, and they... well they rustle up some toast on a Sunday morning if you're lucky. And they're hurt when you don't shower them with lavish praise and possibly a knighthood.

Even the kids will help out around the house from time to time – if the bribes are big enough. But you still love them don't you? You wiped their bottoms when they were small, you nursed them through illnesses, you fed them, clothed them, helped them learn to read and write and then they gave you something in return which is beyond value – a crayon drawing to stick on the fridge.

Oh mum, you must be a saint! You're probably beyond sainthood. We bet St. George never had to breastfeed a baby in a high street department store while getting dirty looks from the staff; we bet St. Patrick never had to break up a jelly throwing contest (otherwise known as a birthday party) between a dozen three year-olds, and we bet Saints Andrew and David never had to compete with other saints at the school gates on what outfits they we were wearing, what car they were driving, and what exotic holiday location they were off to in the half-term.

Mum, we raise our hats and our glasses to you. You're wonderful. In fact, you're the best Mum in the world. Where would we be without you? Well, we wouldn't be here at all would we? You've put up with a lot over the years – the tears, the tantrums, the sleepless nights, then even after going through all that with hubby, you still decided to have children.

You imagined a sweet little baby nestling in your arms, gazing at you adoringly, then sleeping soundly in its little cot with a contented smile on his or her face. Despite all the horror stories from friends, relatives and other cynics you thought somehow that your baby would be different. It was different all right!

But you struggled through, you battled on, you coped and coped again (and again and again) and yes, it was tough, but there were rewards too – what were they again? Oh yes, the hugs, the kisses, bath time fun, bedtime stories, seaside holidays, dropping them off at Grandma's for a couple of days – bliss!

So, Mum, we've decided that what you need now is a good laugh. And we don't mean the sort of laugh that you had when dad said he seriously thought he was doing his share of the household chores, we mean a good old-fashioned belly laugh at the realities of being a mum. And, like we said, it's nice to know you're not alone. Your experience of motherhood is unique, but some things are the same the world over: like the way kids' body clocks are finely adjusted to coincide with yours – i.e. the moment you go to sleep they wake up.

So sit back, put your feet up, and have a good laugh on us. Remember, if you look hard enough at motherhood there's a "ho ho" in there somewhere!

Laugh With Mother

Some things are part of a mum's lot whether they have babies, teenagers or in-betweenies. Hell, some things are part of a mum's lot even when her offspring are middle-aged with grey hair and have kids of their own. That's the thing about motherhood – you never stop being a mum, however much you may want to at times. They say they're going to phone and they forget, they turn up way after meal time and still expect their food to be piping hot, they always befriend the last people you'd want them to, they cause you headaches, heartaches, and don't do your bank balance a lot of favours, but despite everything you still love 'em to bits. Kids eh – who'd have 'em? Mums, that's who.

Q: What is the joy of motherhood?
A: It's what a woman experiences when she's finally got all the children tucked up in bed.

A posh little boy is showing his friends the pictures in his family's photograph album. He turns a page and finds the photos of his mum and dad's wedding. "Ah!" he says. "And these were taken the day that mummy came to work for us."

Have you ever wondered why it is that people who don't have children and people who do each feel sorry for the other?

"It would seem that something which means poverty, disorder and violence every single day should be avoided entirely, but the desire to beget children is a natural urge."

Phyllis Diller

"I know how to do anything. I'm a mom."

Roseanne Barr

"My mum was a lollipop lady – by which I mean she had a very thin body and a big round red sticky head."

Harry Hill

"I treat my mum as a mum and she treats me as a daughter."

Jade Goody (that's sorted that out then)

"So, Carol, you're a housewife and mother. And have you got any children?"

Michael Barrymore (introducing a contestant on a TV quiz show)

"There's a lot more to being a woman than being a mother, but there's a hell of a lot more to being a mother than most people suspect."

Roseanne Barr

"A suburban mother's role is to deliver children obstetrically once, and by car forever after."

Peter De Vries

"My mom is literally a part of me. You can't say that about many people except relatives. And organ donors."

Carrie Latet

"Mothers are all slightly insane."

J D Salinger

"Take motherhood: nobody ever thought of putting it on a moral pedestal until some brash feminists pointed out, about a century ago, that the pay is lousy and the career ladder nonexistent."

Barbara Ehrenreich

"My mother could make anybody feel guilty. She used to get letters of apology from people she didn't even know."

Joan Rivers

"Why do grandparents and grandchildren get along so well? They have the same enemy: the mother."

Claudette Colbert

"By and large, mothers and housewives are the only workers who do not have regular time off. They are the great vacationless class."

Anne Morrow Lindbergh

"Every beetle is a gazelle in the eyes of its mother."

African proverb

Before I became a mother, I had six theories about bringing up children. Now I have six children and no theories.

A mother's prayer:
Lord, Grant me the patience to endure my blessings!

You can fool all of the people some of the time, and some of the people all of the time, but you can't fool Mum!
A mystery about mothers: if a mother's place is supposed to be in the home, why do mums have to spend so much time out in the car driving everyone around?

It's hard for a mum to keep young these days. Especially if she has more than two of the little blighters.

Q: How many Jewish mothers does it take to change a light bulb?
A: Ah! Don't bother, I'll just sit here in the dark. I don't want to be a nuisance to anybody.

There was a little boy called Joshua who was very good to his mum. He hardly ever went home.

There was another little boy who had a difficult relationship with his mum. One day she took him aside... and left him there.

I'd like to be the ideal mother, but I'm too busy raising my kids.

I could be a perfect parent if it weren't for my children letting me down all the time.

A mum says to a fellow mum, "I promised myself that I wouldn't make the same mistakes with my second child that I did with my first – and for the most part I'm not. I'm making entirely new ones."

"If it's five o'clock and the children are still alive, I've done my job."

Roseanne Barr

"Never marry a man who hates his mother, because he'll end up hating you."

Jill Bennett

"She was the archetypal selfless mother: living only for her children, sheltering them from the consequences of their actions... and in the end doing them irreparable harm."

Marcia Muller

"Having someone else to blame when there is a rude smell in the air."

Jane Horrocks (on the advantages of being a mother)

Eddie: "Saffy, Look at Mummy. Look at me. Do I need surgery?"
Saffy: "Yes, have your mouth sewn up."

Absolutely Fabulous

"When your mother asks, 'Do you want a piece of advice?' it's a mere formality. It doesn't matter if you answer yes or no. You're going to get it anyway."

Erma Bombeck

"Mummy, I love you so much that when you die I'm going to have you stuffed."

A small child to his mummy

"My mother's great. She has the major looks. She could stop you from doing anything, through a closed door even, with a single look. Without saying a word, she has that power to rip out your tonsils."

Whoopi Goldberg

Yes, there's nothing like the joy of motherhood. Especially after all the kids have left home.

All You Need To Know About Mothers - As Told By Primary School Children

Why did God make mothers?

She's the only one who knows where the tape is.
Mostly to clean the house.
To help us out of there when we were getting born.

How did God make mothers?

He used dirt, just like for the rest of us.
Magic plus superpowers and a lot of stirring.
God made my mum just the same like he made me. He just used bigger parts.

What ingredients are mothers made of?

God makes mothers out of clouds and angel hair and everything nice in the world and one dab of mean.
They had to get their start from men's bones. Then they mostly use string. I think.

The Seven Ages of Mum

Pregnancy – Nine months of being told horror stories by other mums about giving birth and having the life scared out of you.

Having baby – You thought all those horror stories were exaggerated, and then you go into labour and find they were true!

Bringing up baby – An endless cycle of attention seeking and grumpy behaviour, followed by bottle and sleep – you should have had plenty of practice with your husband.

Bringing up toddler – You've heard of the terrible twos, but they never tell you about the tortuous threes, the flipping fours and the frazzled fives, let alone the sodding sixes, and the stinking sevens do they?

Bringing up child – You think you're going to have a quiet life while they're at school, but then it's preparing lunchboxes, going to sports days, nativity plays, the PTA, meeting with teachers, dropping off, picking up, school trips – when are you going to get your well-earned rest?

Bringing up teenager – Mood swings, door-slamming, furtive behaviour, drunkeness – it's Dad all over again isn't it?

They fly the coop – Ah, despite everything, you're missing them already aren't you?

All In The Family

Families are a bit like fudge. Overall they're very sweet but there's always a few nuts scattered throughout.

I've got lots of distant relatives – especially my mum and my dad.

"Parents like the idea of kids, they just don't like their kids."

Morley Safer

**"Definition of parents: People who bare infants, bore teenagers, and board newlyweds.
Definition of a family: A social unit where the father is concerned with parking space, the children with outer space, and the mother with closet space."**

Evan Esar

"A family is a unit composed not only of children but of men, women, an occasional animal, and the common cold."

Ogden Nash

"I owe a lot to my parents, especially my mother and father."

Greg Norman

"My family is really boring. They have a coffee table book called *Pictures We Took Just to Use Up the Rest of the Film.*"

Penelope Lombard

"When our relatives are at home, we have to think of all their good points or it would be impossible to endure them."

George Bernard Shaw

"In some families, 'please' is described as the magic word. In our house, however, it was 'sorry'".

Margaret Laurence

"The thing that impresses me most about America is the way parents obey their children."

Duke of Windsor

"Parenthood: The state of being better chaperoned than you were before marriage."

Marcelene Cox

"Adam and Eve had many advantages, but the principal one was that they escaped teething."

Mark Twain

"Most children threaten at times to run away from home. This is the only thing that keeps some parents going."

Phyllis Diller

Becoming A Mum

When does a woman become a mum? Well, technically when she gives birth, but all mums know it starts way before that. You could trace the start of motherhood back to the first time somebody commented on your 'bump' (does my bump look big in this?), or even before that, if you're one of those lucky women who maintains a girlish figure throughout her pregnancy. You could trace the start of motherhood back to when you saw the first hospital scan and suddenly realised you're worrying for two now. Maybe you can trace it back to when you first tested positive on that little kit from the chemist's, and began to start thinking about what colour to paint the nursery. But at whatever point you realise you've become a mum you suddenly find you're a member of a very exclusive club. The knowing looks in the maternity waiting room, the rueful 'I know what you're going through' smiles as your baby has a screaming fit in the supermarket; motherhood is an underground network of mutual support, and boy do you need it!

A couple are trying for their first baby. One day the woman takes a pregnancy test which confirms she is pregnant. Straight away they phone up the doctor and book themselves in for an appointment. The doctor examines the woman and everything seems to be fine. Then he takes a small rubber stamp and stamps it on the woman's stomach. The couple have no idea what this was for so when they get home they find a magnifying glass and the man looks to see what it was the doctor stamped on her stomach. "What does it say?" asks the woman. "It says," says the man, "in very tiny letters, 'When you can read this, come back and see me again.'"

"They say men can never experience the pain of childbirth. They can... if you hit them in the goolies with a cricket bat for 14 hours."

Jo Brand

Tee shirt slogan seen being worn by a pregnant woman: *A Man Did This to Me, Oprah*

If motherhood was going to be easy, you know they would never have started it with a thing called labour!

A mum was expecting her third child and was telling the other two that the new baby in her tummy was kicking a lot. She told her eldest little boy that when she had been pregnant with him, he had hardly kicked at all. "You know why that was don't you?" said the little boy. "No. Why?" asked the mum. "Because," he said, "I knew you were my mummy."

"Death and taxes and childbirth! There's never any convenient time for any of them!"

Margaret Mitchell

A boy is given some homework from school on the subject of childbirth. So he goes to his mother and asks, "Mummy, how was I born?" Well, dear," says his mummy slightly embarrassed, "The stork brought you to us." "I see," says the little boy. "And how did you and Daddy get born?" "Well, the stork brought us as well," says his mother. "OK," says the little boy. "So how were Grandpa and Grandma born?" "Er... well... the stork brought them too didn't he?" says his increasingly frustrated mother. A few days later the homework is finished and the little boy hands it in to his teacher who opens it up and reads, "This report has been very difficult to write due to the fact that there hasn't been a natural childbirth in my family for at least three generations."

Starting a family is a bit like having a bath – at first it seems lovely but then after a while it's not so hot.

A teacher asked her class to write a story about a fireman. When she reads the effort that Little Johnny hands in, she is quite confused. "What does this say?" asked the teacher. Little Johnny picks up his essay and reads: "The fireman came down the ladder pregnant." "That's what I thought it said," said the teacher. "Do you know what pregnant means, Johnny?" she asked. "Of course I do," said Johnny confidently. "It means carrying a child."

"If pregnancy were a book they would cut the last two chapters."

Nora Ephron

Martha was a very busy woman. In fact she was so busy she wasn't able to attend the birth of her child.

Tom buys his first house after years of renting and his friend Bill gives him a bottle of champagne as a housewarming present. Unfortunately it gets stored away in a cupboard and forgotten about for years. In the meantime, Tom gets married to Carol and she moves in and they start a family. Having a clear out years later, Tom finds the bottle and thinks it would be a good idea to drink it to celebrate the birth of their third child. The couple are holding a big party, and with all their family and friends gathered around they uncork the bottle to the applause of the assembled guests. Tom proudly reads out the message on the gift tag: "Congratulations, mate. This time it's actually yours."

"I want to have children, but my friends scare me. One of my friends told me she was in labour for 36 hours. I don't even want to do anything that feels GOOD for 36 hours."

Rita Rudner

A little girl says to her mummy, "Wow, Mummy, you're getting really fat!" "Yes," says Mummy. "But don't forget it's because mummy has a baby growing in her tummy." "Well, yes, I know that," says the little girl. "I just wondered what it was you've got growing in your bum?"

Printed in a church bulletin:
Thursday at 5pm there will be a meeting of the Little Mothers Club. All wishing to become little mothers, please see the minister in his study.

> **"When I was born I was so surprised I didn't talk for a year and a half."**
>
> **Gracie Allen**

A pregnant woman involved in a car accident is rushed to hospital where she goes into a coma. She wakes up a month later and notices she's no longer carrying her child so she asks, "Doctor, what's happened to my baby!" "Don't worry," says the doctor. "You've had twins! You're the proud mother of a handsome baby boy and a beautiful baby girl and they're absolutely fine." "Thank goodness for that," says the woman, "But now I'll have to think of names for them." "No need," says the doctor. "While you were in the coma, your brother came into the hospital and named the children for you." "My brother!" shrieks the woman. "Oh no! My brother's a complete idiot! What kind of ridiculous names has he given them?" "Well," says the doctor, "He's named your daughter Denise." "Oh. OK. That's no so bad," says the woman beginning to calm down again after her moment's panic. "And what's he called the little boy?" "Denephew," says the doctor.

> **"My husband and I are either going to buy a dog or have a child. We can't decide whether to ruin our carpet or ruin our lives."**
>
> **Rita Rudner**

Eddie: "Oh, darling, Mummy loves you. On the day you were born I knew I wanted you..."
Patsy: "However, the next day..."

Absolutely Fabulous

A pregnant woman is taken into the maternity hospital about to give birth. "And what about the father?" asks the midwife. "Is he going to be present at the delivery?" "Probably not," says the woman. "He and my husband don't really get along."

Week after week a six-year-old boy keeps coming in to school and telling his teacher all about the new addition expected at his house in a few months time. One day his mother lets the boy touch her tummy so he can feel the movements of the unborn child. The six-year-old looks very surprised at this, but says nothing. The next day at school, his teacher sits the little boy down and says, "So Tommy, what's the latest news on that new baby brother or sister of yours?" "Oh God!" says Tommy bursting into tears. "I think my mummy's eaten it!"

Patsy: "My mother never gave birth... she had something... removed!"

Absolutely Fabulous

There was a middle-aged couple who had two stunningly beautiful blonde teenage daughters. They decided to try one last time for the son they always wanted. After months of trying, the wife became pregnant and, sure enough, nine months later delivered a healthy baby boy. The joyful father rushed to the nursery to see his new son. He took one look and was horrified to see the ugliest child he had ever seen. He went to his wife and said that there was no way he could be the father of that child. "Look at the two beautiful daughters I fathered." Then he gave her a stern look and asked, "Have you been fooling around on me?" The wife smiled sweetly and told him, "Not this time, no."

"The most effective form of birth control I know is spending the day with my kids."

Jill Bensley

A couple go to a prenatal class which is designed for parents who already have at least one other child. The instructor is trying to get the idea over to the parents that the new addition to the family might be a serious issue for their older child. "Some parents," says the instructor, "tell their child, 'We love you so much that we've decided to bring another child into the family.' But think about how that sounds to the child. Ladies, imagine if your husband came home one day and said, 'Honey, I love you so much I decided to bring home another wife.' What would you say to him?" And one of the woman shouts out, "Can she cook?"

"Giving birth is little more than a set of muscular contractions granting passage of a child. Then the mother is born."

Erma Bombeck

A little boy has got into a bad habit of sucking his thumb all the time and it drives his mum crazy. In the end she says to him, "Right! You're sucking your thumb again, are you? Do you know what happens to people who suck their thumbs? I'll tell you. Sucking you thumb makes you fat. You keep doing it you'll get fatter and fatter until you're absolutely enormous and eventually you'll explode." Two weeks later, the little boy is sitting on the bus with his mum and on the seat opposite them is a woman eight months pregnant. The little boy keeps staring at the woman's great round belly until she says to him, "I'm sorry. Do you know me?" "No," says the little boy, "but I know what you've been doing."

A little girl asks her mummy, "Mummy, where do babies come from?" "Babies?" says her mother. "Why, the stork brings babies." "I see," says the little girl. "So who keeps bad people from robbing our house?" "Well, that's obviously the police isn't it, dear," says Mummy. "OK," says the little girl. "So say our house was on fire. Who would come and rescue us then?" "The firemen would come and rescue us if our house was on fire," says Mummy. "Right," says the little girl. "And who grows our food for us?" "The farmers grow our food for us," says Mummy. "OK then," says the girl. "So Mummy..." "Yes, dear," says her mummy. "What is it we need Daddy for again?"

"I think I'd be a good mother. Maybe a little over-protective. Like I would never let the kid out of my... body."

Wendy Liebman

A pregnant woman is at home with her three-year-old daughter. Suddenly, the woman starts to go into labour so she calls for an ambulance. A paramedic turns up, but the baby is due any minute so he decides to deliver it in the house rather than try to get to the hospital. After a lot of pushing the baby is born. It's a boy. The paramedic lifts him by his little feet and spanks him on the bottom to get him crying. Then he gives the baby to the mother. The paramedic turns to the three-year-old girl and asks her what she thinks of her new baby brother. "I don't think he should have crawled in there in the first place," says the girl. "Smack him again!"

"With the birth of each child you lose two novels."

Candia McWilliam

A woman is married to her husband for 15 years and during that time they have 15 children together. In the end there's nothing for it. They decide they have to get a divorce on grounds of compatibility.

Do you know somewhere in the world a woman gives birth to a child every single minute. We've got to find this woman, tell her about the population problem and get her to stop.

> **"It sometimes happens, even in the best of families, that a baby is born. This is not necessarily cause for alarm. The important thing is to keep your wits about you and borrow some money."**
>
> **Elinor Goulding Smith**

The Smiths were having difficulty having children so they decided to use a proxy father to help start their family. They make an arrangement to meet the proxy father, and on the day he is due to arrive, Mr Smith kisses his wife and says, "I'm off. The man should be here soon." Half an hour later, just by chance, a door-to-door baby photographer rings the doorbell, hoping to make a sale. "Good morning madam. You don't know me, but I've come to..." "Oh, no need to explain. I've been expecting you," says Mrs Smith cutting in. "Oh really?" says the photographer. "Well, good! I've made a speciality of babies." "Oh yes," says Mrs Smith. "That's what my husband and I particularly hoped you'd be able to help us with. Please come in and have a seat. Just where do we start?" "OK. Just leave everything to me," says the photographer. "I usually try a couple in the bathtub, then one on the couch and perhaps a couple on the bed. Sometimes the living room floor is fun as well; then you can really spread out." "Bathtub, living room floor?" says Mrs Smith thinking no wonder she never got anywhere trying for a baby with her husband. "Well, madam, none of us can guarantee a good one every time. But if we try several different positions and perhaps from six or seven different angles, I'm sure you'll be pleased with the results." "Er, I hope we can get this over with quickly, gasps Mrs. Smith. "Madam, in my line of work, a man must take his time. I'd love to be in and out in five minutes, but I think you'd be a bit disappointed with that to be honest." "Tell me about it!" thinks Mrs Smith to herself. The photographer opens his briefcase and pulls out a portfolio of his baby pictures. "This one was done on the top of a bus in London," he says showing her the first. "Oh my God!" exclaims Mrs Smith hardly able to believe what she's hearing. "And these twins turned out exceptionally well when you consider their mother was quite difficult to work with," says the photographer handing Mrs Smith another picture. "Difficult to work with?" asks Mrs. Smith. "Oh yes. I'm afraid I finally had to take her to Hyde Park to get the job done right. People were crowding around four and five deep, pushing to get a good look." "Four and five deep?" asks Mrs Smith, eyes widened in amazement. "Yes," says the photographer. "And for more than three hours too. The mother was constantly squealing and yelling. I could hardly concentrate. Then darkness approached and I began to rush my shots. Finally, when the squirrels began nibbling on my equipment I just packed it all in." Mrs Smith leans forward, "You mean they actually chewed on your, er... um... equipment?" "That's right. Well madam, if you're ready, I'll set up my tripod so that we can get to work." "Tripod??" Mrs. Smith now looks extremely worried. "Oh yes, I have to use a tripod to rest my Canon on. It's much too big for me to hold while I'm getting ready for action. Madam? Madam? Oh my goodness, she's fainted!!"

"The child had his mother's eyes, his mother's nose, and his mother's mouth. Which left his mother with a pretty blank expression."

Robert Benchley

A newlywed wife says to her husband when he gets in from work: "I have great news for you. Pretty soon we're going to be three in this house instead of two." The husband can't believe it. He starts glowing with happiness and kisses his wife saying: "Oh darling, that's absolutely wonderful. I'm the happiest man in the world." And the wife says, "I'm glad that you feel that way because my mother is moving in with us tomorrow morning."

Groucho Marx used to present a quiz show on American radio and later on TV. On one show he had a contestant called Mrs Story. He asked her, "How many children do you have?" Mrs Story replied, "Nineteen." Groucho was amazed. "Nineteen?! Why do you have so many children?" he said. "It must be a terrible responsibility and a burden." "Well," replied Mrs Story, "because I love my children and I think that's our purpose here on Earth, and I love my husband." "I love my cigar, too," replied Groucho, "but I take it out of my mouth once in a while!"

"I didn't know how babies were made until I was pregnant with my fourth child."

Loretta Lynn

A husband arrives at the hospital just after his wife has given birth and asks her how it was. "Well," she says, "Grin the biggest, widest grin you can." "OK," says the puzzled husband, grinning from ear to ear. "Is that what it was like?" "Now put a finger in each corner of your mouth and stretch it out just a little bit wider." "OK," says the husband, following her instructions, and wondering where all this is leading. "That's it, wider still," says the wife. "Ow," says the husband, "it's starting to hurt. Is this what it felt like?" "Keep stretching those lips," says the wife. "Ughnn!" says the husband, following her instructions. "Right, now stretch them over the top of your head!"

"My mother says I'm the reason she can't sit down. She blames me for the entire ruination of her body. This is a woman who attempted a tummy tuck in her eighth month of pregnancy."

Ruby Wax

Frequently Asked Questions And Answers For Mums-To-Be

Q: When is the best time to get an epidural?
A: Right after you find out you're pregnant.

Q: Where is the best place to store breast milk?
A: In your breasts.

Q: How does one sanitise nipples?
A: Bathe daily and wear a clean bra. It beats boiling them in a saucepan.

Q: What happens to disposable nappies after they're thrown away?
A: They are stored in a silo to be used in the possible event of global bio-chemical warfare.

Q: I'm two months pregnant now. When will my baby move?
A: With any luck, right after he finishes college.

Q: How will I know if my vomiting is morning sickness or the flu?
A: If it's the flu, you'll get better.

Q: Should I have a baby after 35?
A: No, 35 children is enough.

Q: What does it mean when the baby's head is crowning?
A: It means you feel as though not only a crown but the entire throne is trying to make its way out of you.

Q: Is there anything I should avoid while recovering from childbirth?
A: Yes, pregnancy.

Q: Do I have to have a baby shower?
A: Not if you change the baby's nappy very quickly.

Q: Our baby was born last week. When will my wife begin to feel and act normal again?
A: When the kids leave to go to university.

Q: Am I more likely to get pregnant if my husband wears boxers rather than briefs?
A: Yes, but you'll have an even better chance if he doesn't wear anything at all.

Q: Can a woman get pregnant from a toilet seat?
A: Yes, but the baby would be awfully funny looking.

Q: What is the easiest way to figure out exactly when I got pregnant?
A: Have sex once a year.

Q: My brother tells me that since my husband has a big nose, and genes for big noses are dominant, my baby will have a big nose as well. Is this true?
A: The odds are greater that your brother will have a fat lip.

Q: What is a chastity belt?
A: A labour-saving device.

Q: Since I became pregnant, my breasts, rear end, and even my feet have grown. Is there anything that gets smaller during pregnancy?
A: Yes, your bladder.

Q: Ever since I've been pregnant, I can't go to bed at night without onion rings. Is this a normal craving?
A: Depends on what you're doing with them.

Q: What is the most common pregnancy craving?
A: For men to be the ones who get pregnant.

Q: What is the most reliable method to determine a baby's sex?
A: Childbirth.

Q: My blood type is O-positive and my husband's is A-negative. What if my baby is born, say, type AB-positive?
A: Then the jig is up.

Q: The more pregnant I get, the more often strangers smile at me. Why?
A: 'Cause you're fatter than they are.

Q: My wife is five months pregnant and so moody that sometimes she's borderline irrational.
A: So what's your question?

Q: Under what circumstances can sex at the end of pregnancy bring on labour?
A: When the sex is between your husband and another woman.

Q: How long is the average woman in labour?
A: Whatever she says divided by two.

Q: What's the difference between a heavily pregnant woman and a *Playboy* centrefold?
A: Nothing, if the pregnant woman's husband knows what's good for him.

Q: What is the best time to wean the baby from nursing?
A: When you see teeth marks.

The Mum Spotter's Guide

Yummy mummy
Perfect hair, perfect clothes, perfect make-up – all the signs of wear and tear are showing on the nanny.

Crummy mummy
Dashes into school playground ten minutes late, porridge in hair and skirt tucked into knickers only to then suddenly remember she's left her child at home.

Slummy mummy
Has large storage section under pushchair for bringing home industrial quantities of bargain booze, and has installed a built-in ashtray at the top of the rain hood just above baby's head.

Dummy mummy
Suddenly finds herself with five kids at the age of 22, which is a complete mystery to her as she's never had any sex education whatsoever.

Chummy mummy

She's the one who doesn't want to be like a traditional mother, she wants her kids to be her best mates – especially when they become teenagers. What she forgets however is that when you're a teenager the last person on Earth you want your mates to see you hanging around with is your mum. Especially if your mum has really tried hard to be "down with the kids" and is now sporting tattoos and a full array of facial piercings and her preferred form of transport is a skateboard.

Lumme! Mummy

Permanently "gobsmacked" at the behaviour and demands of her children as if it is a complete shock that babies need attention virtually 24 hours a day and that you don't finally get them off your hands until they're about 35.

Kids' Advice On Romantic Issues

"Tell them that you own a bunch of sweet shops."
Six-year-old boy (On how you can make someone fall in love with you)

"On the first date, they just tell each other lies, and that usually gets them interested enough to go for a second date."
Boy aged ten (on dating)

"No one is sure why it happens, but I heard it has something to do with how you smell. That's why perfume and deodorant are so popular."
Girl aged nine (on falling in love)

"If falling in love is anything like learning how to spell, I don't want to do it. It takes too long."
Boy aged seven (on falling in love)

Mum's Dictionary

Alarm clock – A device used to awaken people who don't enjoy the benefit of small children.

Barbecue – A cooking device that can only be operated by men (the precise opposite of a cooker).

Buggy – Mode of transport for little buggers.

Christmas – Unpaid overtime.

Dinner – The eighth wonder of the world: a meal that makes itself and magically appears at the same time every evening.

Dishwasher – Mum.

Dumb waiter – the man in the restaurant who asks your children if they'd like pudding.

Fairy story – A tale that mums tell children and dads tell mums.

Family planning – A synonym for "never again".

Father – A man who's never around when you need him, but always in the way when you don't.

Feedback – Baby's way of telling you he doesn't like what you've just fed him.

Flowers – A tribal peace offering for both sins committed and yet to be committed.

Full name – What you call your child when you're angry.

Grandparents – The people who think your kids are great even though they don't seem to think you're bringing them up properly.

Hamster – Child's pet, the ownership of which passes temporarily to the mother when the cage needs cleaning out.

Hearsay – What young kids do when anyone utters a rude word.

Homework – Schoolwork for mums.

Impregnable – A woman whose memory of childbirth is still fresh in her mind.

Iron – A despicable four letter word, not be mentioned in polite female company.

Kids' film – Two hours of peace.

Labour – Whatever it is, it sure ain't a party.

Lie-in – Mum's special treat, granted regularly. Every Mothers' Day.

Magic wand – A semi-mystical device with which mothers conjure up meals at any time of day or night by any member of the family uttering the magic words "I'm hungry".

Maternity leave – A frantic period of decorating, hospital visits and shopping for baby clothes and accessories.

Mobile – A clever device that keeps children mesmerised as babies in the cot and then again when they're teenagers.

Nappy – Filling station for babies.

Night out – A semi-mythical event that is heralded by the appearance of blue moons, flying pigs and hell freezing over.

Party – Hell, with jelly and ice cream.

Paternity leave – Golf on full pay.

Potty – A state of mind you're driven to when your toddler doesn't use it.

Pregnancy – A completely unfair additional period of parenthood that the father does not have to suffer.

Prenatal – The good old days before you had children and could do what you wanted.

Puddle – A small body of water that attracts other small bodies into it – especially when they're not wearing wellies!

Relaxation – Sorry, this word does not exist in Mum's dictionary.

School report – An update on how well Mum's getting on with the homework.

Shopping list – A checklist of requirements, carefully worked out and budgeted for and then left at home when actually shopping.

Show-off – Any child that is cleverer/more talented than yours.

Sleepover – Either the most blissful word in the English language or the most hellish depending on whether your kids are visiting or hosting.

Teenager – A changeling that appears mysteriously in your house one day and takes the place of your beloved child.

Telephone – An object whose ownership is passed from one generation to the next without any discernible handover ceremony.

Television – An entertainment device for the whole family that nevertheless only ever seems to show sport or cartoons.

Toddler – A weapon of mass destruction.

Toy – An supernatural object which, however often returned to child's room, will somehow magically reappear in various parts of the house without anyone touching it.

Two-minute warning – When the baby starts pulling faces and making those dreaded straining noises.

Vacuum cleaner – Device that can clean the whole house when used by mums, but can only clean the car when used by dads.

Washing – A task that increases the more you do of it.

Washing machine – One of a small family of mechanical devices that men aren't fascinated by and have no desire to master.

Weekend – That time at the end of the week when everyone, apart from mums, has a rest.

Wine – Special medicine Mummy has to take every night.

Wise Words For Mums

Perhaps the three wisest words you could offer a mother are: don't have kids. But it's a bit late for that now isn't it? And it's a funny thing that all the people most readily available with advice about how to bring up your children are either people who haven't had any, or people who've made a complete hash of it themselves. So, although you may have already had all the advice you could ever want from these child "experts" why not have a sift through these little gems of wisdom – they may be right, they may be wrong, but at least

they might make you laugh, and perhaps, as a mum, that's what you need most of all:
Avenge yourself. Live long enough to be a problem to your children.

If you have any advice to pass on to your children, remember to do it while they're still young enough to think you might possibly know what you're talking about.

There is only one group of people in the world who are sure they know the proper way to raise children: the ones who've never had any.

Don't forget: if you bring your child up to be polite and courteous to everyone at all times, he will never be able to change lanes on a motorway when he grows up.

Small children disturb your sleep, big children your life.

Yiddish proverb

"Parents were invented to make children happy by giving them something to ignore."

Ogden Nash

"Parenthood remains the greatest single preserve of the amateur."

Alvin Toffler

"If you've never been hated by your child, you've never been a parent."

Bette Davis

"There may be some doubt as to who are the best people to have charge of children, but there can be no doubt that parents are the worst."

George Bernard Shaw

"I have found the best way to give advice to your children is to find out what they want and then advise them to do it."

Harry S Truman

"If you can't be a good example, then you'll just have to be a horrible warning."

Catherine Aird

"The value to a child of poor role models is underestimated. Parents have the idea that it is their duty to set a good example, never realising that a bad one will do just as well. Indeed better."

Jill Tweedie

Life is divided into two halves: the first half is when it's ruined by your mum and dad, and the second half is when it's ruined by your flippin' kids.

There are only two things a child will share willingly: communicable diseases and his mother's age.

Money may not be everything, but it sure helps keep the kids in touch when they're older.

For adult education, nothing beats children.

"My childhood should have taught me lessons for my own parenthood, but it didn't because parenting can be learned only by people who have no children."

Bill Cosby

"Having children is like having a bowling alley installed in your brain."

Martin Mull

"The best way to keep children home is to make the home atmosphere pleasant... and let the air out of the tyres."

Dorothy Parker

"As a mother, my job is to take care of the possible and trust God with the impossible."

Ruth Bell Graham

God invented mothers because He couldn't be everywhere at once.

God invented guilt so mothers could be everywhere at once.

Having children will turn you into your parents.

A child's behaviour will improve in proportion to the distance she is away from the parent.

Those who say they sleep like a baby obviously haven't got one.

The art of being a parent is to sleep when the baby isn't looking.

By the time you learn to be a good parent, you're out of a job!

It is easier to build a child than to repair an adult.

Kids are nature's way of saying your house is far too tidy!

Raising children is like being pecked to death by a duck.

Saying "yes" to a child is like blowing a balloon. You have to know when to stop.

A three-year-old will get almost as much fun out of a £350 swing set you buy him as he does out of a small green worm.

The best thing to spend on your children is time.

"Mother's words of wisdom: 'Answer me! Don't talk with food in your mouth!'"

Erma Bombeck

"Things are going to get a lot worse before they get worse."

Lily Tomlin

"My mother used to say that there are no strangers, only friends you haven't met yet. She's now in a maximum security twilight home in Australia."

Dame Edna Everage

"I've noticed that one thing about parents is that no matter what stage your child is in, the parents who have older children always tell you the next stage is worse."

Dave Barry

Remember – never, ever hit your children. Except in self-defence.
A child's enjoyment of a piece popular entertainment will always be in inverse proportion to his or her parent's enjoyment of it.

The chance of a surprise visit by your parents-in-law is directly proportional to the size of the mess in your home.

Two is equal to two, except when referring to time. Two minutes of tantrum lasts 20 times as long as two minutes of quiet time.

A baby will inevitably wake up in the wee-wee hours of the morning.

The face of a child can say it all, especially the mouth part of the face.

A youth becomes a man when the marks he wants to leave on the world have nothing to do with tyres.

Celibacy is not hereditary.

"Children are the most expensive form of entertainment."

Mihaela Iosof

"Raising kids is part joy and part guerrilla warfare."

Ed Asner

"Never lend your car to anyone to whom you have given birth."

Erma Bombeck

"Any kid will run an errand for you, if you ask at bedtime."

Red Skelton

"In order to influence a child, one must be careful not to be that child's parent or grandparent."

Don Marquis

"The one thing children wear out faster than shoes is parents."

John J. Plomp

"Children begin by loving their parents; after a time they judge them; rarely, if ever, do they forgive them."

Oscar Wilde

"The truth is that parents are not really interested in justice. They just want quiet."

Bill Cosby

"Familiarity breeds contempt - and children"

Mark Twain

Children are natural mimics who act like their parents despite every effort to teach them good manners

The advice your son rejected is now being given by him to your grandson.

All mothers are working mothers.

There is only one pretty child in the world, and every mother has it.

If you want your children to listen to you, try talking softly to someone else.

Your children will be a great comfort to you when you reach old age. Unfortunately they will help you reach it more quickly.

Children never put off till tomorrow what will keep them from going to bed tonight.

There's only one way to bring kids up right – but unfortunately nobody's found out what it is yet.

Parents often talk about the younger generation as if they didn't have anything to do with it.

"Even when freshly washed and relieved of all obvious confections, children tend to be sticky."

Fran Lebowitz

"What is a home without children? Quiet."

Henny Youngman

"Do your kids a favour. Don't have any."

Robert Orben

"The hand that rocks the cradle is the hand that rules the world."

William Ross Wallace

"All women become like their mothers. That is their tragedy. No man does. That's his."

Oscar Wilde

We Love You, Mum!

Some Of The Reasons People Give For Why They Love Their Mums

One reason I love my mum is because she gave birth to me!

And if she hadn't she wouldn't be your mother would she? Alternatively, if she hadn't remembered to give birth to you she'd now be walking round massively pregnant as a result of being several years overdue.

My mother is always there for me!

Of course Mum's always there for you! It's no good for your mum to try to hide from you, is it? You've got her name, and address, and everything!

And if she really did try and escape somewhere you couldn't find her, you would be very well placed to give the police a good description of her, and even a DNA sample remarkably similar to hers!

If it wasn't for my mum I wouldn't be here at all!

That may be true, but let's not forget the important (albeit very brief) role in your creation played by your father. And of course he wasn't the only one responsible, was he? No. Who could forget that Saturday evening long ago, that particularly inspiring edition of *Match of the Day* and that even more inspiring six cans of beer.

But on Mother's Day do anyone's kids ever think to send flowers to the players of Manchester United and the man who invented Watney's Red Barrel?

She's the only person in the world I can talk to.
You're going to have an extremely limited social life then, aren't you?

My mother made a lot of sacrifices for me!
What do you think your mum is? Some kind of druid?

She's the only person who really understands me.
The only poor person who has no real excuse to escape from your self-pitying whining, you mean.

My mum is my best friend!
What? You mean your mum hangs around in the local supermarket car park with you on Saturday nights, drinking cheap cider and trying to pick up members of the opposite sex?

Actually, I suppose there must be some mums out there somewhere that do just that...

She's been my rock.
There you are, Mum. They think you're hard, grey and several million years old.

She's always there when I need her.
This makes Mum sound like directory enquiries doesn't it? Or perhaps a public convenience.

My mum is beautiful, both inside and out
This is surely an opinion that can only be verified by a gynaecologist.

Preparing For Motherhood...

To make sure you are fully aware of the joys that motherhood will bring, please try the following:

- To give you an idea of what pregnancy will be like, put on a dressing gown and shove a bag stuffed full of tennis balls down the front.
- Walk around with this for nine months. Then at the end of this period, remove about ten per cent of the tennis balls.
- Next, drink four litres of water in rapid succession before getting a friend to have a good rummage through your bag of tennis balls. This will help you appreciate what it will be like to have a small person sitting on top of your bladder for the next nine months while using it intermittently as a bouncy castle or water bed.
- Invite complete strangers to put their hands on your tummy to see if they can feel your digestive processes working. This is what they will do to feel your baby moving when your bump starts growing. The only difference is that then you won't need to ask them.
- Make sure there's plenty of sweet and savoury food mashed into the back seat of your car and the remains of sticky half chewed sweets pressed into every ashtray and other cubby hole you can find.
- Have a conversation with another adult. Enjoy that? Good. It's going to be a few years before you get to do that again.
- Dissolve a small amount of urine, faeces and vomit in a half litre of water. Put this mixture into a vaporiser and go round spraying every room in your house with it. This is what the place will smell like for the next two and a half years. Then try spraying it all over yourself before meeting friends and see if you can spot any changes in the way they react to you.
- Get a friend to constantly run their fingers down a blackboard for several hours each day. This is almost, but not quite, as bad as a baby screaming its head off.
- As for the way the rest of your breasts will feel, simply go to a very poorly recommended cosmetic surgeon and have him temporarily enlarge them to Jordan-like proportions.

- To give an inkling of one of the results of breastfeeding you may experience, take two pieces of sticky tape and carefully attach one to each of your nipples. Tear the pieces of sticky tape off and then attach a fresh couple of pieces. Keep doing this for the next eight hours then finally buffer to a finish with sandpaper.
- When you go to bed at night set up 15 alarm clocks to go off at irregular intervals to make sure you never get longer than half an hour's sleep. Just to make sure your sleep pattern is properly disturbed, each time you are woken up read a short book aloud, sing a few songs or dance around the room for a few minutes while hugging a large cuddly toy.
- Switch on every radio and TV in the house at full volume. Then try reading a reasonably complicated book. This will give you some idea of what your concentration levels will be like after childbirth.
- To get an idea of what it's like getting little kids to do what you ask, try going up to a complete stranger and giving them a series of orders in a language you have just made up and which they are therefore very unlikely to understand.
- Then go to your local supermarket, take out your purse and empty it all straight into their till. Do this every couple of days.
- Every time you visit your local supermarket get into a screaming argument with another shopper. After getting very flustered in front of everyone in the shop, try and end the argument by buying the other shopper some sweeties.
- Communicate only in baby language even when talking to other adults.
- Get complete strangers to lecture you in detail on where you're going wrong in everything you try to do. Once you have children, they will do this all the time on all aspects of childcare.
- Find a couple who already have children and lecture them in detail on where they're going wrong in every aspect of their childcare. That's the very last time you'll seem to have any of the right answers on that subject.

- To get an idea of what shopping will be like with small children in tow, hire a couple of baboons from the local safari park and take them with you round your local large department store. Make sure to visit the glassware department with them.
- When out with a friend pick them up and sniff their pants every half an hour to see if they need changing.
- For an idea of what meal times will be like once they're on solids, get a liquidizer, pack it full it to the brim with soft, squashy food, place it in the middle of your dining table and then switch it on for five minutes without making any attempt to put the lid on it.

So Are You Sure You're Ready To Be A Mum?

Mess Test

Smear peanut butter on the sofa and curtains.

Place a fish finger behind the couch and leave it there all summer.

Stick your fingers in the flower bed. Then, rub them on the clean walls. Cover the stains with crayons.

Craft Skills Test

Take an egg carton. Using a pair of scissors and pot of paint, turn it into an alligator.

Now take the tube from a roll of toilet paper. Using only Scotch tape and a piece of foil, turn it into an attractive Christmas candle.

Lastly take a milk carton, a ping-pong ball, and an empty packet of Cocoa Pops. Make an exact replica of the Eiffel Tower.

Congratulations! You have just qualified for a place on your local play group committee.

Toy Test

Obtain a 55 gallon drum of Lego bricks. If these are not available, you may substitute tin tacks. Wait in the bedroom, whilst a friend spreads them all over the house. Put on a blindfold. Try to walk to the bathroom or kitchen. Do not scream, as this could wake a child at night.

Supermarket Test

Borrow one or two small animals (goats are best) and take them with you on your next weekly shop. Always keep them in sight, and pay for anything they eat or damage.

Feeding Test

Obtain a large plastic milk jug. Fill halfway with water. Suspend from the ceiling with a stout cord. Start the jug swinging. Try to insert spoonfuls of soggy cereal (such as Honey Nut Loops or Cheerios) into the mouth of the jug, while pretending to be an airplane. Now dump the contents of the jug on the floor.

Dressing Test

Buy an octopus and a small bag made out of loose mesh. When the octopus is unhappy (it will turn bright red), attempt to put it into the bag so that none of its tentacles hang out.
Time allowed: all morning.

Transport Test

Forget the BMW and buy a family car. And don't think that you can leave it out in the driveway spotless and shining. Family cars don't look like that.

Buy a chocolate ice cream cone and put it in the glove compartment. Leave it there. Get a 50 pence piece, and stick it in the CD player. Take a family size pack of chocolate biscuits. Mash them into the back seat. Run a garden rake along both sides of the car.

There. Perfect.

If Men Got Pregnant...

Maternity leave would be about seven years long.

Birth would always be done under general anaesthetic.

Hospital delivery rooms would have a bar in one corner.

Most families would only have one child (I'm not going through that again!).

The world population crisis would be solved at a stroke.

Morning sickness would rank as the nation's number one health problem.

Natural childbirth would never ever happen.

Women would be expected to be the bread winners and do the housework as well (hey, I've got a baby to look after!).

Coffee mornings would be held at the pub.

No one would notice the bump - they'd just assume they were professional darts players.

They'd suddenly get strange food cravings like chips with curry sauce or pickled eggs (oh, hang on, that's their usual diet anyway).

They'd probably try to start "anti-natal" classes.

All methods of birth control would be improved to be 100 per cent effective.

Before And After Children

Before children I slept like a baby.
After children I don't sleep like a baby and even the baby doesn't sleep like a baby.

Before children I had a life.
After children I have a life sentence.

Before children I shared candlelit dinners with my husband.
After children I share candlelit birthday cakes with 12 screaming kids.

Before children I had a lie-in at weekends.
After children I don't even notice it's the weekend.

Before children I had a figure to die for.
After children I have a figure to diet for.

Before children my life was full of happiness.
After children my life is a full of nappy mess.

Before children my bank balance was in the black and I was in the pink.
After children my bank balance is in the red and I'm blue.

Before children I had an active social life.
After children I have a hyperactive toddler.

Before children I refused to leave the house without make-up.
After children I refuse to leave the house without checking my hair for porridge.

Before children I was happy with my lot.
After children my lot are driving me to drink.

Before children I regularly bought new things for the house.
After children I regularly have to replace things round the house.

Before children I had a job and a future.
After children I have a job thinking about the future.

Before children my husband brought me home flowers and chocolates.
After children my husband brought me home from the maternity unit.

Before children I had a floor you could see your face in.
After children I have a face you can see some flaws in.

Before children I was a bit of a looker as a woman.
After children I have the look of a bitter woman.

Mums And Babies

How can this little bundle that barely weighs more than a couple of bags of sugar dominate your life so much – and when will it ever end? After several months of fractured sleep and cleaning up messes of one kind or another you will probably swear that if another person says, “it will get easier you know”, you’ll punch them. Even worse, if someone says, “it’ll get worse before it gets better”, you may possibly kill them and feel it will be justifiable homicide. But then there are those moments of maternal bliss when baby is gurgling contentedly with a smile on its chubby little face, or finally snuggled up warm and safe and fast asleep – OK, it may be 3.30am but you've got to be grateful for small mercies.

"You can sort of be married, you can sort of be divorced, you can sort of be living together, but you can't sort of have a baby."

David Shire

"My friend has a baby. I'm recording all the noises he makes, so later I can ask him what he meant."

Steven Wright

"An ugly baby is a very nasty object, and the prettiest is frightful when undressed."

Queen Victoria

Of course, as the poet said, "Out of the mouths of babes and sucklings comes all manner of things." Usually this happens shortly after feeding time.

One day, shortly after the birth of their new baby, the mother has to go out and do some errands. The proud father stays at home to watch his wonderful new son. Soon after the mother goes out though, the baby starts to cry. The father does everything he can think of doing, but the baby still won't stop crying. Finally, the dad gets so worried he decides to take the infant to the doctor. After the doctor listens to the father relate all that he has done to get the baby to stop crying, he examines the baby's ears, chest and then checks his nappy. When he undoes the nappy, he finds that it's completely full. "Ah, you idiot!" says the doctor. "Here's your problem! Why haven't you just changed his nappy? It's completely full!" "No no! That doesn't need changing yet," says the dad. "Look what it says on the pack. They're good for up to ten lbs!"

The baby is crying so a wife says to her husband, "Could you change our son for me?" A couple of hours later he's back, looking very pleased with himself, holding a baby girl.

A not too bright couple are delighted when the adoption centre calls them and tells them have a Russian baby for them to adopt. On the way home they stop at the local further education college and sign themselves up on a course to learn Russian. "Are you going on holiday to Russia?" asks the registration clerk. "No," they reply. "We've just adopted a Russian baby and when he starts talking we want to know what he's saying."

"If your baby's 'beautiful and perfect, never cries or fusses, sleeps on schedule and burps on demand, an angel all the time,' you're the grandma."

Theresa Bloomingdale

"The worst feature of a new baby is its mother's singing."

Kin Hubbard

"Baby: An alimentary canal with a loud voice at one end and no responsibility at the other."

Elizabeth Adamson

"A baby's a full-time job for three adults. Nobody tells you that when you're pregnant, or you'd probably jump off a bridge. Nobody tells you how all-consuming it is to be a mother – how reading goes out the window, and thinking too."

Erica Jong

Babies are nature's way of showing people what the world looks like at 2am.

Definition of a baby: a handy way of disposing of unwanted cash and filling up free time, while cutting down on unnecessary sleep, curtailing a demanding social life, and curing a neurotic obsession with person hygiene.

A woman has twins, and gives them up for adoption. One of them goes to a family in Egypt and is named "Amal." The other goes to a family in Spain, they name him "Juan". Years later, Juan sends a picture of himself to his mum. Upon receiving the picture, she tells her husband that she wished she also had a picture of Amal. Her husband responds, but they are twins. If you've seen Juan, you've seen Amal."

"My mother loved children, she would have given anything if I'd been one."

Groucho Marx

"The hand that rocks the cradle usually is attached to someone who isn't getting enough sleep."

John Fiebig

"A tip to all new mothers: Don't put your baby in bed with you because you might fall asleep, roll on it and put your back out!"

Harry Hill

"I always wondered why babies spent so much time sucking their thumbs - then I tasted baby food."

Robert Orben

"No animal is so inexhaustible as an excited infant."

Amy Leslie

"A baby is a blank cheque made payable to the human race."

Barbara Christine Seifert

"I married your mother because I wanted children – imagine my disappointment when you came along."

Groucho Marx

"I don't know why they say 'you have a baby.' The baby has you."

Gallagher

A young woman was showing off her new-born twins to a friend of the family who asked if she ever had any trouble telling them apart. "No, I've not really had much problem," she said, and held them up one at a time, "This one's Benjamin, and this is Elizabeth."

A little boy has a new baby brother and is listening to him screaming up a storm. He asks his mum, "Where did you get him from?" His mother replies, "You know very well where I got him. He came from heaven." "Yeah," says the little boy. "Well, I can see why they threw him out!"

A little boy is watching his mummy breastfeeding his new baby sister. After a little while he asks, "Mummy, why have you got two of those? Is one for hot and one for cold?"

My parents were so proud of my looks when I was a baby that they used to pretend I'd been kidnapped just so they could see my picture in the papers.

Linda, a harassed mother, answers the phone in her house. A voice on the other end says, "Hello, dear. It's Mummy." Linda says, "Mummy! Thank God you rang. I'm having a terrible day. The baby spilt prune juice over the carpet. Now he won't have his afternoon nap. The washing machine is broken, the repair man is three hours late, the fridge is empty, there's nothing for tea and I have a terrible headache." "Calm down," says Mum. "Let your mother sort it all out for you. I'll tell you what. I'll come straight over. On the way I'll get some food for dinner, some pain killers for your headache. I know an easy way to get juice stains out of the carpet, and I'll send the baby fast asleep with one of my famous lullabies. After that, I'll make us dinner while you wait for the repair man to get there. And while all that's going on, you can have a nice sit down and put your feet up until John gets home." "John?" says Linda. "What do you mean John?" "Your husband," says Mum. "No," says Linda. "My husband's name is Bob." "Oh," says the voice over the phone. "Is that 457 889?" "No," says Linda. "You've dialled 347 889." There's a few seconds' pause before Linda asks, "So does this mean you're not coming over?"

Two little boys are talking. One says, "I had a nightmare last night. I dreamt that Dolly Parton was my mother." "What's wrong with that?" asks the second little boy. And the first replies, "In my dream I was a bottle-fed baby."

The choice of your child's best friend before they start school will correspond directly to the distance the friend lives from your house.

A mum was carrying her 18-month-old baby in a backpack when she had to rush to catch a bus. Unfortunately in her hurry to get to the bus stop in time she missed her footing and fell down a flight of 13 steps, still with the baby strapped on her back. She ended up bruised, bleeding and with her trousers torn but obviously she was most concerned about the baby. Luckily the baby turned out to be uninjured. Not only that immediately after the tumble down the steps the mum heard a little voice from behind her say, "Again!"

"I had a traumatic childhood. I was breast-fed from falsies."

Woody Allen

"I came from a very big family. There were so many wet nappies in the kitchen there was a rainbow in the lobby."

Les Dawson

"We spend the first twelve months of our children's lives teaching them to walk and talk and the next twelve telling them to sit down and shut up."

Phyllis Diller

"Every baby born into the world is a finer one than the last."

Charles Dickens

A four-year-old little boy knows all about breastfeeding from observing her mother feed his little sister. So whenever he sees a large chested woman anywhere, he always says, "Look at that lady, mummy. She's very full, isn't she?"

A young woman takes a baby to the doctor's. "He seems to be ill," she says. "Instead of putting on weight, he's lost four ounces in the last few days." The doctor examines the baby and then asks the woman whether the baby is being breast fed or bottle fed. "Breast fed," she says. "All right then," he says, "let's have a look at them. Strip to your waist." So the woman takes her top and bra off and the doctor squeezes both breasts, massages them a little and then pinches her nipples. "Hmm, well I'm not surprised the baby's losing weight – you're not producing any milk whatsoever, young lady." "Well no, I wouldn't be, would I?" says the woman buttoning her shirt back up. "Seeing as I'm the baby's auntie!"

A young couple arrive back home with their new baby. "Hey, I've got an idea," says the new mum. "Why don't you try changing the baby's nappy." "Nahh," says the dad. "I'm a little bit busy at the moment. I'll tell you what though, you do this one, I'll do the next one." A few hours pass by and the baby's nappy needs changing again, so again the new mum asks the new dad to lend a hand. "No, sorry," he says. "You misunderstood. I didn't mean the next nappy. I meant the next baby."

The ease with which a toddler acquires the ability to say a word increases with its likelihood to embarrass a sailor.

A woman goes to her psychiatrist. "Doctor, I can't sleep at night," she says. "I have this terrible fear I won't hear the baby if he falls out of his cot in the next room. What can I do?" "Oh well, that's easy," says the doctor. "Take the carpet off the floor. You should hear him then."

A six-year-old little boy sees his mother breastfeeding his eight month old sister and asks, "Mummy, did you feed me like that when I was a baby?" "Yes," answers his mum. "Wow!" says the little boy. "I bet I really enjoyed that."

A Yorkshire couple have five children; Jack, Tom, Jessica, Sophie and Mao Tse Tung. Obviously Mao Tse Tung is a bit of an unusual name for someone from Yorkshire but the couple didn't think they had any choice because they'd read that every fifth baby born in the world is Chinese.

I keep thinking to myself, if I wanted to hear the pitter-patter of little feet, why didn't I just put some shoes on the cat?

When Peter was four, his mum had another baby, and understandably he was a bit jealous. After a few months Mum explained to Peter that because they now had another baby growing up in the house they'd probably have to move to a bigger place. "I don't think it will work, Mum," said Peter. "What do you mean?" asked Mum. "Well, now she's crawling she'll probably follow us."

Mum comes home one day with her blouse open and her left breast hanging out. "What's happened to you?" asks her worried husband indicating her state of disarray. "Oh no!" says the mum. "I must have left the baby on the bus!"

Things Mums Don't Want To Hear From Their Partners During Childbirth...

So do you think the baby will come before Match of the Day starts?

If you think this hurts, I should tell you about the time I twisted my ankle playing football.

That was the kids on the phone. Did you have anything planned for dinner?

Could you do that last contraction again? I don't think I got it on the camcorder.

Hey you know what? When you lay on your back, you look like a python that's swallowed a wild boar.

Wow! You should see the colour you've turned.

You don't need an epidural. Just relax and enjoy the moment.

All the guys from the pub are just outside. You don't mind if they come in and watch for a bit do you?

I am absolutely appalled by the language I've heard from you tonight. So just stop your swearing and breathe.

Your nurse is quite pretty isn't she?

Oops! Which cord was I supposed to cut?

Hey! Your stomach still looks like there's another one in there.

Guess what! I've already texted a picture of you in that position to everyone in my phone book.

Oh by the way. I forgot to mention, I've just been made redundant and we're six months behind on the mortgage.

Do you know, after thinking about it, I'm not sure I'm ready to cope with the demands of fatherhood.

Advice From Kids On Romantic Issues

"Yell out that you love them at the top of your lungs... and don't worry if their parents are right there."

Boy aged eight (on how you can make someone fall in love with you)

"One way is to take the girl out to eat. Make sure it's something she likes to eat. French fries usually works for me."

Nine-year-old boy (on how you can make someone fall in love with you)

"I think you're supposed to get shot with an arrow or something, but the rest of it isn't supposed to be so painful."

Boy aged eight (on falling in love)

"Most men are brainless, so you might have to try more than once to find a live one."

Girl aged ten (on how women can select their life partner)

Do's And Don'ts Of Naming Your Child

Don't think that because a film star can get away with naming their child Apple or Satchel that you can too – remember that in Hollywood all kids have strange names so strange is normal.

Don't follow the alleged example of the Beckhams in naming your child after the place they were conceived – "Isle of Dogs" is going to be a challenging name for any child, especially a girl, and don't even think about "Back Seat Of The Vauxhall Astra"

Do consider the acronym your child's full name may spell out – Peter Robert Andrew Trotter, Tiberius Ibrahim Thompson and Sabrina Loretta Angela Gibbings are not going to thank you in later years... especially not when they're at school.

Don't name your child after all the members of your favourite football team, especially now they have so many foreign players – they'll be forever overrunning official forms when they grow up.

Don't invent names yourself – think of Frank Zappa's poor offspring being named Dweezil and Moon Unit.

Don't do a George Foreman and give all your children the same name (in his case, George). Ok, it'll make life easier when you start to lose your marbles, but it'll be damned confusing in the meantime.

Do remember that the poor child will have to live with that name for the rest of its life, and while Pixie Fou Fou might be a cute name for a three-year-old with pink ribbons in her hair, it won't go down so well with a 60-year-old judge.

Things I Learned From My Mum

My mum taught me patience:
"Just you wait till your father gets home."

My mother taught me achievement:
"You have driven me to my wit's end!"

My mother taught me multi-tasking:
"Sit up straight, eat your dinner, and behave yourself."

My mother taught me mathematics:
"I want you to do it by the time I've counted to ten."

My mother taught me about contortionism:
"Wow! Just look at the dirt on the back of your neck."

My mother taught me about Trappist monks:
"I don't want to hear another word out of you."

My mother taught me professional acting:
"Now say sorry like you mean it."

My mother taught me ballistics:
"This place looks like a bomb's hit it."

My mother taught me praise:
"You really know how to show me up, don't you?"

My mother taught me about overcoming disability:
"If you cut your toes off with that lawn mower, don't you come running to me."

My mother taught me fortune-telling:
"You're going to live to regret that."

My mother taught me about the inter-connection between meteorology and physiognomy:
"You keep pulling that face, the wind's going to change and you'll be stuck like that."

My mother taught me about rewards:
"Boy, have you got it coming to you."

My mother taught me self-awareness:
"You don't know you're born."

My mother taught me about the circle of life:
"I brought you into this world and I can take you out of it again."

My mother taught me about helping others:
"If you don't wipe that silly grin off your face, I'll do it for you."

My mother taught me power dressing:
"If you don't pull your socks up you'll let the whole family down."

My mother taught me selfishness:
"Eat it up, half the world's starving."

My mother taught me about swearing an oath:
"I swear I will kill you."

My mother taught me wildlife observation:
"Your room looks like a pigsty."

My mother took me about rural life:
"Do you want to shut that door? Were you born in a field?"

My mother taught me about justice:
"You know, one day you're going to have kids, and I pray they turn out exactly like you!"

Ten Good Things About Adopting Kids

Whatever negative traits they have, no one can blame it on your genes, and if they display any positive traits you can claim it's all down to your wonderful mothering skills.

You can stop in their tracks those people who lean over the pram and say 'ooh, he's got your eyes'.

You don't have to go through all the hassle of carrying the baby for nine months, and the agony of childbirth.

You don't even have to go to all the trouble of thinking up a name.

You can feel rather smug that while you had to attain certain rigorous standards before you could become a mother, most people have absolutely no qualifications at all.

When they get to that age where they start asking 'where did I come from?' you can tell them precisely, and at what exact time.

When they do anything wrong you can really confuse people by saying 'I blame the mother'.

You can completely avoid the sleepless nights, "terrible twos" and the potty training by adopting a child when it's a bit older.

You can choose when to start a family rather than being forced into it by some unfortunate drunken accident.

You don't have to wait for Mr Right, and you definitely don't have to settle for Mr Wrong before you can have a child.

You Know You're A Mum When...

- The last time you went out with your husband for the night was to a school open evening.
- Your idea of indulgence is scraping out the jelly bowl after the kids' tea.
- You start fancying the actors in kid's TV programmes.
- You go straight to the children's section when you enter a bookshop.
- You say, "Look, a moo cow!" even when you're in the car with adults.
- Your idea of financial success is being just a bit overdrawn at the bank.
- You start looking forward to your evening glass of wine at about 11am.
- You first find yourself saying something your mum used to say to you.
- You get excited about meeting a girlfriend for coffee.
- You start looking forward to going back to work.
- You occasionally wonder what that strange, unfamiliar sound is, and you realise it's silence.
- You only look in the mirror to check that you still exist.
- You suddenly feel as if you've turned into Snow White – your entire daily schedule revolves round a bunch of midgets.
- Getting through a whole night without being woken is worthy of an entry in your diary.
- The washing machine is running 24 hours a day.

- You spend more of a meal time issuing instructions than you do actually eating.
- You have a crunchy floor.
- You actually welcome door-to-door salesmen as you crave being able to talk to another grown-up.
- The only tape you can find to play in the car is on the Early Learning Centre label.
- You get to 11am and suddenly realise you forgot to have breakfast.
- You eat your toast off a bright orange plastic plate.

Mum's Buzzword Bingo

Give your children each a card with the following phrases on it. Each time they hear one of them, they cross it off their card. The first one to cross off all the phrases shouts "Bingo!" and is declared the winner.

Look at the state of you.

I'm at the end of my tether.

Because I said so.

This place looks like a pigsty.

Don't forget to wash behind your ears.

Don't answer back.

You wait till your father gets home.

Do you have any idea what the time is?

I don't care what time your friends go to bed.

If you don't eat up you won't grow big and strong.

I'm sick of telling you...

Father Christmas doesn't bring toys to naughty little children.

I'm going to count to ten...

You've really done it this time.

If I'd spoken to my mother like that...

This place won't clean itself you know.

Get up those stairs this minute!

How To Spot The Mother Of A Toddler

Haggard face with dark rings under eyes.

Bits of breakfast cereal in hair.

Knees in trousers worn from kneeling down to talk to toddler.

Handbag full of tissues, gummy sweets and emergency food and drink supplies.

Forever glancing at watch because real life has to be crammed into a tiny window between nursery drop-off and pick-up.

She never looks you in the eye because she's always looking at ground level to see what the little so and so is up to now (even when he's not there).

If anyone spills anything she's immediately got a choice of wet wipes or tissues at the ready.

Even the inside of her car is untidy.

Mums And Little Kids

It's true, kids do say the funniest things. Like "Mum, why don't you work, like Daddy?" Grrr! Or "Mum, can I have a little brother or sister?" No, dear, Daddy's chopped down the gooseberry bush and the stork's knackered. Yes, once children get to the age of about two they suddenly turn into quiz show hosts: "Why is grass green?", "Where do babies come from?", "why do we only have one nose, but we've got two ears?" Can I phone a friend? You could try, but your friends are probably just as stumped as you are. Bringing up toddlers is like trying to train wild animals. Wild animals that ask lots of questions. You thought things would get easier when they could learn to walk, but you forgot that when they can walk they can also run – usually out of the shop when you're still searching for your purse at the till. And if they're not running away, they're running rings round you. But you wouldn't be without out them would you? Well maybe, just for a couple of hours – long enough for a soak in the bath or a grown-up lunch, or perhaps a weekend in Paris...

The golden age in life is when the kids are too old to need baby-sitters but too young to borrow the family car.

Definition of a young child: a noise with dirt on it.

A five-year-old little boy told his mother, 'When you were my age, you was just a baby!'"

During the filming of an early silent movie version of *Oliver Twist* in 1922, the star of the film, child actor Jackie Coogan, was required to cry on cue at a certain point in the script. The moment at which Coogan had to start blubbing was when one of the boys in the orphanage with him asked, "Where's your muvver?" The clue obviously should have been in the fact that the conversation was being held in an orphanage. Nevertheless Coogan found great difficulty in shedding real tears on camera. Eventually the film's director, Frank Lloyd, came up with a ruse and told the little boy to imagine that his mother really had died. Jackie Coogan tried thinking of this but it still didn't reduce him to tears. In the end he came up with an alternative solution of his own and asked the director, "Mr Lloyd, would it be all right if I imagine my dog has died?"

> **"Youngsters of the age of two and three are endowed with extraordinary strength. They can lift a dog twice their own weight and dump him into the bathtub."**
>
> **Erma Bombeck**

A little boy is being tucked up in bed by his mummy. A thunderstorm is raging outside. "Mummy," says the little boy, "Can I sleep in your bed with you tonight?" "No," says Mummy, "I have to sleep with Daddy." "That's not fair," says the little boy. "Can't you tell the big coward not to be such a baby!"

"Hands up," says a teacher, "Who can tell me the name of the Speaker of the House?" A little boy puts his hand up and says, "It's Mummy!"

A mum met a psychologist at a party and tried to get some free professional advice. "So," said the mum, "what kind of toy do you think would be best to get for a little boy on his third birthday?" "Well," said the psychologist, "first of all I'd need to know a bit more about the child." "OK," said the mum, "Say it's for a child who's very bright, very quick-witted and quite exceptionally advanced for his age. And say he has good coordination and is able to express himself very well for his age..." "Oh, I get it now," interrupted the psychologist. "It's YOUR child!"

An American mum is driving her little girl to her friend's house for a play date. "Mommy," the little girl asks, "how old are you?" "Hey!" says the mum, "you don't ask a lady her age. It's not polite." "OK," the little girl says, "How much do you weigh?" "Now really," the mother says, "these are personal questions and are really none of your business." Undaunted, the little girl asks, "OK so why did you and Daddy get a divorce?" "Those are enough questions!" says the exasperated mother walking away and leaving the little girl to play with her friend. "My mom wouldn't tell me anything," the little girl tells her friend. "Well," says the friend, "all you need to do is look at her driver's licence. It is like a report card, it has everything on it." Later that night the little girl says to her mother, "I know how old you are, you are 32." The mother is surprised and asks, "How did you find that out?" "I also know that you weigh 140 pounds." The mother is in shock now. "How in heaven's name did you find that out?" And," the little girl says triumphantly, "I know why you and Daddy got a divorce." "Oh yeah?" says the mother. "And why's that?" "Because you only got an F in sex!"

"Have you any idea how many children it takes to turn off one light in the kitchen? Three. It takes one to say, 'What light?' and two more to say, 'I didn't turn it on.'"

Erma Bombeck

A little girl had a pain in her ear and went to help herself to a painkiller tablet from the bathroom cabinet. She found the bottle of pills but then tried and tried to get the lid off but to no avail. Finding what she was up to, her mum explained that the pills could be dangerous. The bottle had a childproof cap so Mum would have to open it for her. "But, Mum," asked the little girl, "how did the bottle know it was me?"

A frantic mother phones up the doctor's surgery and says, "Doctor, I'm really worried. My little boy Kieran has swallowed a whole bottle of headache pills. What shall I do?" "Well," replies the doctor, "firstly, calm down. Now, is he having hot flushes?" "No," says the woman. "Is he drowsy?" "No," she says. "Does his face look pale?" "No." "Has he been sick?" "No. But a whole bottle of headache pills. Isn't there something we should do?" "Well," says the doctor, "if you're really concerned, you could try giving him a headache."

"I'm glad I'm finally eight. This is the oldest I've ever been in my entire life!"

An eight-year-old little boy

You know why kids brighten up any household? They never turn the lights off.

A three-year-old boy put his shoes on all on his own. Unfortunately he'd got things slightly wrong and his mum said to him, "Oh dear! Look! You've put your shoes on the wrong feet." "Don't be silly?" said the little boy. "Those are my feet aren't they?"

No wonder kids are confused today. Half of all adults tell them to find themselves; the other half tell them to get lost.

Three-year-old little Jimmy is being given a bath by his mum. She's just washing his hair and says to him, "Wow, your hair is growing really fast! I think you need another hair cut already." And little Jimmy says to her, "Yeah well maybe you should stop watering it so much."

A Jewish mother is walking down the street with her two young sons. A passer by stops to admire them and asks how old they are. "The doctor is three," the mother answers, "and the lawyer is two."

A little girl is sitting at home one day, typing like mad on the computer. Her mummy asks her what she's doing and she says, "I'm writing a story." "That's nice," says Mum, "What's it about?" "I've no idea," says the little girl. "I can't read."

A mum was studying to be a nurse and so was reading up on the subject of haematology. Her four-year-old daughter asked her what she was reading and she told her that she was learning about blood and went on to explain about how the heart pumps blood all the way round the body. She concluded this basic introduction to the working of the human body by showing her daughter how she could feel her own pulse in her wrists and feet. A bit later the mum noticed her little girl was looking at the soles of her feet and then twisting, turning and pulling down her shorts to try and look at her bottom. "What are you doing?" asked the mum. "I'm trying to find where we put the batteries," said the little girl.

Little Freddie's mum turns to Little Freddie's dad and says, "Do you know it's such a nice day, I think I'll take Little Freddie to the zoo." "No. I wouldn't bother doing that," says his dad. "If the zoo wants him, let the zoo come and get him!"

> **"Oh, what a tangled web do parents weave, when they think their children are naive."**
>
> **Ogden Nash**

The persons hardest to convince they're at retirement age are children at bedtime.

Hollywood superstar John Travolta was, as little boy, greatly indulged by his mother who thought he could do no wrong. One day Mrs Travolta was watching young John take out the garbage and remarked to his older sister, "Look at him. He's a borderline genius."

A little girl goes up to the desk at her local library and hands over a book to take out. The librarian looks at the book and is concerned to see that it's called, *Advice for Young Mothers*. "Oh," says the librarian. "Why do you want to take this book out?" "Isn't it obvious?" says the little girl. "I collect moths."

"The real menace in dealing with a five-year-old is that in no time at all you begin to sound like a five-year-old."

Jean Kerr

A girl and her mummy and daddy are flying off on holiday. The family have a seat which overlooks the plane's wing. As they near their destination, the plane banks to one side so giving them all a view over the sea. "Look," says the mother to her little daughter as she points out of the window, "Can you see the water?" The girl tries peering over the wing and says, "No. But I think I can see the diving board."

A little girl is given a one pound coin by her mother. A little while later, the mother asks the girl if she'll be saving her money up to buy something special. "Oh. I don't have that pound any more," says the girl. "I gave it to an old lady I saw in the park." "Oh you kind-hearted child!" says her mother. "You mean you really gave that whole pound you had to a poor suffering old woman. I think that's absolutely wonderful! Here! Here's two pounds for being such a very good little girl." So little girl takes the money from her mummy and skips off again. A few minutes later she's back. Her mother asks her where she's been. "I went to see the old lady again and gave her my two pounds," says the girl. "And this time she gave me an even bigger ice-cream."

Q: What is the definition of a vest?
A: Something a little boy wears when his mother feels cold.

A woman sees a group of children playing a game of cricket in the street. She notices that one poor little boy is sitting crying his eyes out in the middle of the children. So the woman goes over to comfort the little boy and picks him up. One of the other children shouts, "Hey, what are you doing? Put him back! He's the wicket!"

Mum Record Breakers: The Youngest Mum Ever

Lina Medina was a Peruvian girl born in the Andean town of Ticrapo in September 1933. She achieved unwanted fame by becoming, at just five years old, the youngest confirmed mother in medical history.

At first it had been presumed that Lina was suffering a stomach tumour but on being taken to Dr Gerardo Lozada it was discovered Lina was in fact seven months pregnant.

Lina it seems had had her first period aged just eight months and had developed breasts by the age of four. On 14th May 1939, at the age of five years, seven months and twenty-one days, she gave birth to a son. Not only that but 14th May that year was Mother's Day.

Her son was born by Caesarian and named Gerardo after her doctor. He grew up believing Lina to be his sister until the truth was revealed to him when he was 10 years old.

It was never determined who the father of Lina's child was although her father was jailed on suspicion of incest but then released because of lack of evidence.

Lina it seems is still with us now aged 74. Gerardo sadly died aged 40 of a bone marrow disease. Lina's second son was born in 1972.

More recently in 2006 a ten-year-old girl from Charleroi in Belgium gave birth to a child, the father of which was revealed to be a 13-year-old boy from her school.

I was quite insecure as a child. I once asked my mother if my father loved me and she told me, "Of course Daddy loves you. He's on Prozac. He loves everyone."

A woman was trying to leave to go away on a work conference, but her seven-year-old daughter kept clinging on to her and crying. She didn't know what had brought on this outburst until she heard the little girl saying to her daddy, "Daddy, I have a loose tooth. If it comes out while Mummy is gone, are you sure you know how to handle this tooth fairy thing?"

A mother is showing her little boy how to zip his coat up. "Here's the secret," she says. "You get the left part of the zip to fit into the other side before you try to pull it up." And the boy looks up at her and says, "OK. So why the hell does that have to be a secret?"

I used to wet the bed when I was little, but my mother came up with an instant cure. She bought me an electric blanket.

A mum and her friend took her little daughter to a movie for her birthday. After leaving the cinema the friend asks the little girl how old she was. "I can't tell you," said the little girl. "I have my mittens on!"

> **"Do not, on a rainy day ask your child what he feels like doing, because I assure you that what he feels like doing, you won't feel like watching."**
>
> **Fran Lebowitz**

A ten-year-old little girl is celebrating her birthday and her mum decides it's time to set up a savings account for her. The little girl was really pleased and because it was going to be her very own bank account, the mum let her fill in the application form herself. When she looked at the form later however, mum noticed that where it asked for the name of the applicant's former bank her daughter had written, "Piggy".

Dad has taken little nine-year-old Kirsty to have her ears pierced for the first time. When they get home and Mum opens the door she takes one look at her little girl and cries out in horror. "Oh my God! What have you done? Look at her!" Kirsty has not only had her ears pierced, she's got a ring through her nose, a stud on her chin, and piercings through her eyebrows. She looks at Dad as if she were going to kill him. "Why did you let them do this to our little girl?" she demands. "Well," says Dad, "They had a special offer on."

"I'm not an oxymoron!"

Seven-year-old

A little boy was going on his first ever trip on a train. He was amazed by the whole experience of travelling by rail. Then the train turned a bend and went into a tunnel. The little boy gave a gasp of surprise at the sudden darkness outside. A few moments later the train rushed out into the daylight again and the little boy remarked, "Hey! It's tomorrow!"

A little boy walks sleepily into his mum and dad's bedroom one night and asks if he can have a story. "Tommy," says his mum, "It's 1.30 in the morning!" "Oh please, Mum," he says, "Can I have a story?" "I've got a better idea," says Mum, pulling back the duvet, "you get into bed with me and when your dad eventually comes home I think we'll be both get to hear a story!"

A mum overheard her two young sons after she'd put them to bed for the night. The seven-year-old whispered to his five-year-old brother, "Tell me when you're asleep, OK?"

Jimmy was at his big sister's wedding when he asked his mum how it was that women were allowed to marry 16 men. "Sixteen?" asked his mum "How do you arrive at that figure?" "Well," said Jimmy, "the vicar said 'four richer, four poorer, four better, four worse.'"

A mother who worked delivering meals to the elderly sometimes used to take her daughter with her while she did her afternoon deliveries. The little girl was fascinated by all the devices she saw in the houses they visited, such as walking sticks, walking frames and wheelchairs. But then one day one of the old people had left their false teeth soaking in a glass. The little girl was amazed. She turned to her mummy and said, "Wow! The tooth fairy is never going to believe this!"

Little David gets separated from his mother in a department store and when he eventually spots her he shouts out "Karen! Karen! Here I am, Karen!" His mother is of course overjoyed to find him but says, "You shouldn't really call me Karen though dear, you should call me Mummy." "But I couldn't do that," says David. "Why not?" asks his mum. "Well most of the other ladies in this place are called 'Mum' too."

A woman who was off work on maternity leave called in to see her old workmates one day, bringing with her the new baby and her seven-year-old son. Everyone gathered around to see the baby, and heard the little boy ask, "Mummy, can I have some money to buy a drink?" "What do you say?" asked the mum. Respectfully, the boy replied, "You're thin and beautiful." On hearing which the woman reached into her purse and gave her son the money.

> **"You don't really understand human nature unless you know why a child on a merry-go-round will wave at his parents every time around - and why his parents will always wave back."**
>
> **William D. Tammeus**

A mother was driving with her three small children in the back of the car on a warm summer's evening when a women in the vehicle in front of them stood up waving, revealing herself to be naked. One of the kids piped up from the back seat, "Mummy, that lady isn't wearing a seat belt!

A little girl asks her mum, "Mum, are the people next door really poor?" "I don't think so, dear," says the mum, "why do you ask that?" "Well," says the little girl, "their baby just swallowed a 50 pence piece and they're making a terrible fuss about it."

A mum was getting fed up waiting for her little girl to choose so in the end she told her she had to make up her mind. The little girl looked up at her and asked, "How do you put make up on your mind?"

> **"For centuries, people thought the moon was made of green cheese. Then the astronauts found that the moon is really a big hard rock. That's what happens to cheese when you leave it out."**
>
> **Boy aged 6**

A six-year-old little girl saw some flowers in a cemetery and said to her mum, "Wow! I wish someone we knew would die so we could leave them flowers."

Little Tommy goes to the dentist and he is told that he has a cavity. "Now," says the dentists, "we need to get that filled straight away. What sort of filling would you like?" "Chocolate and banana."

> **"When I go to heaven, I want to see my grandpa again. But he better have lost the nose hair and the old-man smell."**
>
> **Boy aged 5**

A new neighbour was being introduced to the little girl she had moved in next-door to and asked her, "Do you have any brothers or sisters?" "No," replied the little girl, "I'm the lonely child."

When his friend comes to visit, little Faron takes him up to the bathroom and shows him the bathroom scales. "What is that for?" asks his friend. "It's a bit like a lie-detector," said Faron, "Every time Mum stands on it, she says 'I don't believe it, I don't believe it.'"

A seven-year-old little girl found out where her mum and dad had hidden her presents ready for Christmas day but was caught peeking at them. Mum was about to scold her but the little girl said, "I didn't look much. I've only got little eyes!"

Dad's trying to think of something little Trixie can buy her mum for Christmas. "Hmm, we always get her chocolates. What can we get for a change?" asks Dad. "I know," says little Trixie, "Let's get her some of that old lady stuff." "What old lady stuff?" asks dad. "You know, that special cream she puts on to stay looking young: Oil of Old Lady."

"And lead us not into PlayStation"
Four-year-old boy

A three-year-old girl was looking round a toy shop with her mum. The mum had told her she could choose a present for herself but the toys she kept pointing out were really expensive. "No," said the mum as the little girl asked for yet another highly priced item, "I told you, I've got enough to buy you a small toy today but all the ones you've picked up so far have been really expensive." "So," said the little girl, "why don't you get some expensive money?"

A little girl asked her mother, "Can I go outside and play with the boys?" Her mother replied, "No, you can't play with the boys, they're too rough." The little girl thought about it for a few moments and asked, "If I can find a smooth one, can I play with him?"

A mother was driving her eight-year-old daughter to visit her grandparents. It was late in the evening and there wasn't much traffic on the road. So it was a far cry from the usual mad rush when mum drove her to various appointments in the city. The little girl was sitting thinking during the journey and in the end piped up to say, "Mum, can I ask you something." "Yes," said the mum. "What do you want to know?" "When you're driving," said the little girl, "are you ever the idiot?"

Dad is sitting watching TV one evening when suddenly little William asks the question he's been dreading: "Dad, where did I come from?" "Ask your mother," says Dad. Mum looks annoyed and says, "I think we should both explain it to him." So Dad reluctantly goes into the front room with Mum and they get down the family medical dictionary and an encyclopaedia and go through the whole thing with him in words he can understand. Finally Mum asks "Does that make sense to you dear?" "Yeah, I think so Mum," says William, "but my friend Asif from school said he comes from India, and I wondered where I come from?"

> **"Kids have little computer bodies with disks that store information. They remember who had to do the dishes the last time you had spaghetti, who lost the knob off the TV set six years ago, who got punished for teasing the dog when he wasn't teasing the dog and who had to wear girl's boots the last time it snowed."**
>
> **Erma Bombeck**

A little girl came back from school one day and asked her mother straight out, "Mummy, what's sex?" "OK," said her mother taking the plunge and sitting her daughter down before giving her the little speech she had been mentally planning for some time. She went through the birds and bees and then more specifically about eggs and sperm and what happens when two people love each other very much. At the end of all this the little girl was looking more confused than ever. "What's the matter?" asked her mum. "Didn't you understand any of that?" "I did," said the little girl taking her school bag and pulling out a registration form she had to fill in, "but how am I going to fit all of that into this little box?"

A five-year-old little girl came home from school and told her mother, "Mum, guess what? We learned how to make babies in school today." The mother, more than a little surprised, tried to keep her cool. "That's interesting," she said. "How do you make babies?" "It's simple," replied the girl. "You just change 'y' to 'i' and add 'es'."

A mum is telling her little girl what it was like when she was a child. "We used to skate outside on the pond. I had a swing made from a tyre hanging from a tree in our back yard. And we had a pony which I used to ride across the fields." "Wow," says the little girl. "I really wish I'd got to know you a bit sooner."

Little Jocasta is at a wedding with her mum and is fascinated by all the clothes and the ceremony. "Mum," she says, tugging at her mother's sleeve, "why does the bride have to wear white?" "Well," says mum, "she wears white because... well because it's bright and cheerful and it shows that it's the happiest day of her life." "So," replies Jocasta, "why's the groom wearing black then?"

A little girl was out with her mother when they met a rather wrinkly elderly lady that her mum knew. The little girl looked at the old lady for a few moments and then asked, "Why doesn't your skin fit your face?"

"Everyone is guilty at one time or another of throwing out questions that beg to be ignored, but mothers seem to have a market on the supply. 'Do you want a spanking or do you want to go to bed?' 'Don't you want to save some of that pizza for your brother?' 'Wasn't there any change?'"

Erma Bombeck

A mum took her young son to visit his grandmother one day. The little boy asked the old lady, "Grandma, do you know how you and God are alike?" "No," said the grandma thinking this was a promising basis for a comparison. "How are God and me alike?" "You're both really old," said the little boy.

A little boy was eating breakfast one morning and got to thinking about things. "Mummy, Mummy," he asked, "Why has Daddy got so few hairs on his head?" "That's because he thinks an awful lot," replied his mum, feeling very pleased with herself for coming up with such a good answer to explain her husband's baldness. The boy thought about this for a moment and then asked, "So why do you have so much hair?"

Jemima is looking closely at her mum one day. "Mum," asks Jemima. "Why have you got grey hairs on your head?" "Ah well, you know why that is, don't you," says Mum. "That's because every time a little child does something naughty, one of their mummy's hairs turns grey." "Wow," says Jemima. "So you must have been really naughty when you were little then." "Why do you say that?" asks Mum. "Because look at granny. All her hairs are grey."

"But deliver us some email."

Four-year-old girl

A little girl asked a woman how old she was. The woman answered, "Thirty-nine and holding." The child thought for a moment before saying, "OK. So how old would you be if you let go?"

A little boy told his mum, "I love you so much, Mummy, when you die, I'm going to bury you outside my bedroom window."

Grandparents are similar to a piece of string: always handy to have around, and easily wrapped around the fingers of grandchildren.

A seven-year-old and a five-year-old were at a family party and were overheard as they discussed one of the adult guests. "I bet he's forty," said the seven-year-old. "No, he's eighty," said the five-year-old. "Eighty five!" said the seven-year-old. "No, he's one hundred!" said the five-year-old. "Don't be stupid," said the seven-year-old. "Of course he's not a hundred. That's when you die!"

"My younger brother asked me what happens after we die. I told him we get buried under a bunch of dirt and worms eat our bodies. I guess I should have told him the truth, that most of us go to hell and burn eternally, but I didn't want to upset him."

Boy aged 10

A little girl is asking her mother about God, and as children do, asking lots and lots of questions. "Mummy, is God a man or a woman?" asks the girl. "Well dear," says the mum, "God is both a man and a woman." "I see," says the girl, "So is God black or white?" "God is both black and white dear," says her mum. The little girl thinks about this and then asks, "So is God gay or straight?" Mother is a bit flustered by this and says. "Er, well, er, I suppose he or she is gay or straight." "Oh right," says the girl. "So what you saying is God is Michael Jackson!"

"Our Father, who art in heaven, Harold be thy name..."
Traditional young child's misquote of the Lord's prayer

"And forgive us our trash baskets as we forgive those who put trash in our baskets."

Four-year-old

Grandma is reading a little girl a bedtime story. Half-way through, the little girl interrupts and asks a question. "Grandma," she says. "Did God make you?" "Yes of course," says her grandma. "And did he make me too?" asks the little girl. "He made you too," says her grandma. "So why is your hair white and your skin so wrinkly?" asks the little girl. Her grandmother answers, "Because God made me a long time ago and you he made only a few years ago." "OK. I see," says the little girl. "So he's getting better with practice."

A little boy is talking with his mummy. "Why does God make it rain?" he asks. Mummy replies sagely, "God makes it rains so it will fall on the plants and the plants will grow." "Oh yeah?" says the boy. "So why does he have to make it rain on the pavement as well?"

Songs About Mums

Mamma Mia - Abba
Ma, He's Making Eyes At Me – Lena Zavaroni
Ma Baker – Boney M
Mother – John Lennon
Momma's Little Girl – Paul McCartney
Momma Miss America – Paul McCartney
Mother of Mine – Neil Reid
Mother and Child Reunion – Paul Simon
Mama Weer All Crazee Now – Slade
Mama Told me Not to Come – Three Dog Night
Mama – Spice Girls
Mama, I'm Coming Home – Ozzy Osbourne
Mother Nature – Nat King Cole
Mother's Talk – Tears For Fears
Ma-Ma-Ma-Belle – ELO
Mama Said – Metallica
Mama – Connie Francis
Mama – Genesis
Mama – Kim Appleby
Mama Said Knock You Out – LL Cool J
Mama Used To Say – Junior
Mama – Who Da Man – Richard Blackwood
Mrs Brown You've Got a Lovely Daughter – Herman's Hermits
Mama's Boy – Suzy Quatro
Mama's Pearls – Jacksons

Kids' Buzzword Bingo

Give your mum and dad each a card with the following phrases on it. Each time they hear you say one of them they cross it off. The first one to cross off all the phrases shouts "Bingo!" and is declared the winner.

Why do I have to?
It's not fair!
I hate you!
All my friends are allowed to.
I hate school!
It wasn't me.
I did it yesterday.
You can't make me.
You're so embarrassing!
Why is always me who has to do it?

The Toddler's Rules

If it is on, I must turn it off.

If it is off, I must turn it on.

If it is folded, I must unfold it.

If it is a liquid, it must be shaken, then spilled.

If it a solid, it must be crumbled, chewed or smeared.

If it is high, it must be reached.

If it is shelved, it must be removed.

If it is pointed, it must be run toward with at top speed.

If it has leaves, they must be picked.

If it is plugged, it must be unplugged.

If it is not trash, it must be thrown away.

If it is in the trash, it must be removed, inspected, and thrown on the floor.

If it is closed, it must be opened.

If it does not open, it must be screamed at.

If it has drawers, they must be rifled.

If it is a pencil, it must write on the refrigerator, monitor, or table.

If it is full, it will be more interesting emptied.

If it is empty, it will be more interesting full.

If it is a pile of dirt, it must be laid upon.

If it is stroller, it must under no circumstances be ridden in without protest. It must be pushed by me instead.

If it has a flat surface, it must be banged upon.

If Mummy's hands are full, I must be carried.

If Mummy is in a hurry and wants to carry me, I must walk alone.

If it is paper, it must be torn.

If it has buttons, they must be pressed.

If the volume is low, it must go high.

If it is toilet paper, it must be unrolled on the floor.

If it is a drawer, it must be pulled upon.

If it is a toothbrush, it must be inserted into my mouth.

If it has a tap, it must be turned on at full force.

If it is a phone, I must talk to it.

If it is an insect, it must be swallowed.

If it doesn't stay on my spoon, it must be dropped on the floor.

If it is not food, it must be tasted.

If it IS food, it must not be tasted.

If it is dry, it must be made wet with drool, milk, or toilet water.

If it is a car seat, it must be protested with arched back.

A Mother's Resolutions

When I forget to go to the grocery store, I will not boil the macaroni necklaces my children made for me at nursery school.

I will pack the kids' lunch boxes the night before so I don't throw in a slab of frozen lasagne as they're running for the bus and tell them, "It'll defrost by lunch. If not, you can suck it like an ice lolly."

I will resist the urge to explain to strangers why my son is wearing winter boots, a bathing suit bottom, and an inside-out and backward pyjama top. I will be grateful that he is able to dress himself.

I will always protect the rights of my children, especially their right to remain silent.

When my husband and I go to a restaurant without the kids, I will not roll up his sleeves or move the knives from his reach. I will not accompany him to the bathroom and remind him to wash his hands with soap. If my husband wants dessert at the end of the meal, I will not tell him it depends on his behaviour.

I will learn to accept the outbursts and tantrums as a part of life. After all, I promised to love my husband for better or worse.

When I'm tired of hearing "Mummieeeeee!" a thousand times each day, I will resist changing my name to "Please pass the spinach" or "TV is boring, I'd rather read."

Letter From The Tooth Fairy

Dear ________________ :

Thank you for leaving your tooth/teeth (delete as applicable) under your pillow last night.

Whilst we make every effort to award monetary compensation for children's lost teeth, we were unable to process your application for the following reason(s):

( ) the tooth/teeth could not be located.
( ) it was not a human tooth.
( ) pieces of bone from the Sunday joint do not count as teeth.
( ) the tooth has been deposited at least once before.
( ) it was not one of your teeth.
( ) we were unable to get close to the tooth due to an extremely unpleasant odour.
( ) you were overheard maintaining that you do not believe in the tooth fairy.
( ) snacks provided for the tooth fairy were either unsatisfactory, or absent.
( ) the tooth is still in your mouth and we do not perform extractions.

( ) the tooth fairy does not award cash for fingernail clippings.
( ) your tooth has been forwarded to the Nerve Ending Fairy for appropriate action.
( ) no night light was on at the time of our visit.
( ) you were aged 12 or older at the time your request was received.
( ) the tooth was being guarded by a ferocious fairy-eating dog at the time of our visit.
( ) we discovered evidence of amateur tooth extraction as follows:
[ ] blood-stained string
[ ] pliers
[ ] junior hacksaw
[ ] hammer marks
[ ] chisel marks
[ ] explosives
[ ] portion of skull attached to tooth

We appreciate your request which, on this occasion, we were unable to fulfil but we look forward to visiting you again in the future.

Yours sincerely, The Tooth Fairy

Changing Attitudes In Motherhood:

Swallowing Coins

1st child: When first child swallows a coin, you rush the child to the hospital and demand x-rays.
2nd child: When second child swallows a coin, you carefully watch for the coin to pass.
3rd child: When third child swallows a coin you deduct it from his pocket money!

Your Clothes

1st baby: You begin wearing maternity clothes as soon as your GP confirms your pregnancy.
2nd baby: You wear your regular clothes for as long as possible.
3rd baby: Your maternity clothes are your regular clothes.

The Baby's Name

1st baby: You pore over baby-name books and practice pronouncing and writing combinations of all your favourites.
2nd baby: Someone has to name their kid after your great-aunt Mavis, right? It might as well be you.
3rd baby: You open a name book, close your eyes, and see where your finger falls. Hey Presto? That'll do!

Baby's Dummy

1st baby: If the dummy falls on the floor, you put it away until you can go home and wash and boil it.
2nd baby: When the dummy falls on the floor, you squirt it off with some juice from the baby's bottle.
3rd baby: You wipe it off on your shirt and pop it straight back in.

Preparing For The Birth

1st baby: You practice your breathing religiously.
2nd baby: You don't bother practicing because you remember that last time, breathing didn't do a thing.
3rd baby: You ask for an epidural in your eighth month.

Clothes For Baby

1st baby: You prewash your newborn's clothes, colour-coordinate them, and fold them neatly in the baby's little bureau.
2nd baby: You check to make sure that the clothes are clean and discard only the ones with the darkest stains.
3rd baby: Boys can wear pink, can't they?

Worries

1st baby: At the first sign of distress – a whimper, a frown – you pick up the baby.

2nd baby: You pick the baby up when her wails threaten to wake your firstborn.
3rd baby: You teach your 3-year-old how to rewind the mechanical swing.

Activities

1st baby: You take your infant to Baby Gymnastics, Baby Swing, and Baby Story Hour.
2nd baby: You take your infant to Baby Gymnastics.
3rd baby: You take your infant to the supermarket and the dry cleaner.

Going Out

1st baby: The first time you leave your baby with a sitter, you call home five times.
2nd baby: Just before you walk out the door, you remember to leave a number where you can be reached.
3rd baby: You leave instructions for the sitter to call only if she sees blood.

At Home

1st baby: You spend a good bit of every day just gazing at the baby.
2nd baby: You spend a bit of every day watching to be sure your older child isn't squeezing, poking, or hitting the baby.
3rd baby: You spend a little bit of every day hiding from the children.

Nappies

1st baby: You change your baby's nappy every hour, whether they need it or not.
2nd baby: You change their nappy every two to three hours, if needed.
3rd baby: You try to change their nappy before others start to complain about the smell or you see it sagging to their knees.

You Know You're A Mum When...

- You automatically double-knot everything you tie.
- You find yourself humming the *Spongebob Squarepants* song as you do the dishes.
- You hear a baby cry in the grocery store, and you start to gently sway back and forth, back and forth. However, your children are at school!
- You actually start to like the smell of strained carrots mixed with apple sauce.
- You weep through the scene in *Dumbo* when his mum is taken away, and let's not even begin on what happens when you try to watch Bambi...
- You get soooo into crafts you contemplate writing a book called *101 Fun Crafts to do with Dryer Lint and Eggshells*.
- You spend a half hour searching for your sunglasses only to have your teenager say, "Mum, why don't you wear the ones you pushed up on your head?"
- You are out for a nice meal with your friends, enjoying some real adult conversation, when suddenly you realize that you've reached over and started to cut up their steaks!
- You count the hundreds and thousands on each of your kid's iced doughnuts to make sure they're absolutely equal.
- You only ever have enough time to shave one leg at one sitting.
- You hide in the bathroom to be alone.
- You consider finger paints to be a controlled substance.

- You've mastered the art of placing large quantities of pancakes and eggs on a plate without anything touching.
- You cling to the high moral ground on toy weapons only to find your child has chewed his toast into the shape of a gun.
- You hope tomato ketchup is a vegetable, since it's the only one your child eats.
- You can't bear the thought of your son's first girlfriend.
- You hate the thought of his wife even more.

Advice From Kids On Romantic Issues

"If it's your mother, you can kiss her anytime. But if it's a new person, you have to ask permission."

Boy aged six (on kissing)

"It's never okay to kiss a boy. They always slobber all over you. That's why I stopped doing it."

Girl aged ten (on kissing)

"I know one reason kissing was created. It makes you feel warm all over, and they didn't always have electric heat or fireplaces or even stoves in their houses."

Girl aged eight (on kissing)

"The law says you have to be eighteen, so I wouldn't want to mess with that."

Boy aged seven (on kissing)

"He is trying to steal her chewing gum!"

Six-year-old boy (commenting on a couple who he had seen kissing one another)

Mum's Household Hints

Every mum has her own little supply of tricks of the trade, short cuts and dodges, as well as various make do and mend, search and destroy strategies. Some were handed down by her own mother and some were developed over many years of finding necessary survival techniques just to keep her head above the water of the overflowing bathtub of life. Let's face it, housework is a never-ending chore, and even if you ever did get to the end of it you'd sit back, put your feet up and breathe a sigh of relief as you lay your head on a soft cushion – and then notice that the ceiling needed dusting.

Cleaning your house while your kids are still there is like shovelling your driveway during a snowstorm.

There are three ways to get something done. You can either do it yourself, you can hire someone else to do it, or you can forbid your children to do it.

The best way to keep flies out of the kitchen is to put a pile of cow dung into the dining room.

Tell your husband that tonight you want it to be just like the first day you got married – get him to do the washing up

A child will not spill on a dirty floor.

The one job your husband will do is put the rubbish out, so to save yourself from some housework tell him that all the rubbish has been hidden around the house.

To get your husband to use the washing machine more often, buy one with a remote control and he'll never let you near it

Next time you see an advert for a kitchen gadget that will "cut your housework in half", buy two!

If you ever find your child choking on an ice cube, there is no need to panic. Just pour a jug of boiling water down the child's throat and the ice cube will quickly dissolve.

What's the quickest way to open a jar with a tight lid? Put it on the table and tell the kids to leave it alone.

Next time you're tearing your hair out trying to produce a fancy pudding for a dinner party just remember that "desserts" backwards is "stressed".

Kids' Ideas Of Being Helpful Round The House

If there's one thing worse than Dad and the kids not helping around the house, it's Dad and the kids helping round the house and getting it hopelessly wrong. Yes Dad, it was very good of you to unload the dishwasher this morning and put all the crockery away in the cupboards but you might have noticed that someone (no names mentioned) forgot to turn it on last night, so not only do I now have to reload the dishwasher, I have to clean the grease and leftover food out of the cupboards as well. And kids, it was absolutely lovely of you to bring me tea and toast in bed on Mothers' Day, but tea is usually made with hot water and toast is not normally buttered on both sides.

Opening the door on the washing machine for Mum when she puts the dirty clothes in.

Offering Mum the best seat on the sofa when they're going out for the evening.

Covering the bedroom floor with dirty clothes so she needn't do the hoovering.

Leaving tissues in their pockets so they'll get washed along with their clothes.

Leaving their skateboards at the top of the stairs so "Mummy can have a nice ride".

Bringing insects into the house so they won't eat Mummy's flowers.

Not eating all their food so some of the starving people in the world can have some.

Making the apples nice and shiny – with furniture polish.

Putting cheese in the toaster so Mummy can make toasted cheese sandwiches.

Putting their clothes away in the drawer – even when they're dirty.

Helping Mummy try to find her temper that she's always losing.

Wearing their clothes in the bath to save Mummy having to wash them.

Putting cat food on the windows so that the cat will lick them clean.

Keeping the food bill down by refusing to eat most of what is put in front of them.

Giving Mum their precise destination when leaving the house – "out".

Reducing the parent/child communication barrier by limiting their vocabulary to just three words: "yeah," "nah", "mstarving".

Mum's Daily Schedule

Perfect mother	Slightly imperfect mother	Mother who should not be allowed near children
Get up and make a healthy breakfast	Get up and let the kids choose their own breakfast	Stay in bed while children set light to the kitchen. The firemen will get them some breakfast when they turn up
Walk children to school and collect items for nature study on way	Hustle kids into car at last minute and blow the environment	Tell them to shut the front door quietly as they make their way out into the traffic on their own, then snuggle down under the duvet so you can get back to sleep without having to hear the ambulance sirens
Spend day catching up on cooking, washing, cleaning, home improvements and preparing educational after-school activities	Spend day catching up on daytime TV shows about cooking, washing, cleaning, home improvements and educational after-school activities	Spend day catching up on previous record for day's intake of booze and fags
Supervise homework, piano lessons and home-cooked tea	Download homework off internet, TV and microwaved tea	Give them some money for burgers and chips and tell them you don't what to see them till bedtime
Bath, story and bed	Bath (if there's time), story (if there's time), bed	Whatever

Mum's Household Woes

We've all heard of Sod's Law and Murphy's Law, but what about Mum's Law? This is the unwritten set of rules ensuring that the moment you get in the bath, someone will need the loo; the moment you finish cleaning the kitchen floor someone will walk across it in muddy boots, and the moment you finally drop off into blissful sleep the baby will wake up and bawl its head off. The only mystery is who wrote these rules. It has been observed by more than one mother that whoever it was, it certainly wasn't a woman.

"If evolution really works, how come mothers only have two hands?"

Milton Berle

"Any mother could perform the jobs of several air-traffic controllers with ease."

Lisa Alther

"Everybody wants to save the earth; nobody wants to help Mom do the dishes."

P.J. O'Rourke

"Neurotics build castles in the air, psychotics live in them. My mother cleans them."

Rita Rudner

"I'm not going to vacuum 'til Sears makes one you can ride on."

Roseanne Barr

"Nature abhors a vacuum. And so do I."

Anne Gibbons

"My idea of superwoman is someone who scrubs her own floors."

Bette Midler

"Don't cook. Don't clean. No man will ever make love to a woman because she waxed the linoleum: 'My God, the floor's immaculate! Lie down, you hot bitch!'"

Joan Rivers

Working mothers are guinea pigs in a scientific experiment to show that sleep is not necessary to human life.

I like hugs and I like kisses,
But what I really love is help with the dishes!

Mum has one special labour-saving device in the house that is better than all the others put together – it's called "tomorrow".

Housework is something you do that nobody notices until you don't do it.

They've been treating me like one of the family, and I've stood it as long as I can!

Why is it that just when kids are old enough to make a useful contribution to the housework they don't want to do it any more?

Why is it that the gas repair man always comes when you're out but the electricity meter reader always calls when you're at home?

"I think housework is the reason most women go to the office."

Heloise Cruse

"Every time I close the door on reality it comes in through the windows."

Jennifer Unlimited

"My second favourite household chore is ironing – my first being hitting my head on the top bunk bed until I faint."

Erma Bombeck

"When it comes to housework the one thing no book of household management can ever tell you is how to begin. Or maybe I mean why."

Katharine Whitehorn

Mum is complaining to her friend about having to go out to work and do all the house work too. "Before I go to work I make the children's school lunches, I clean the kitchen and give the bathroom a quick clean, then when I get home from work I clean the rest of the house, and then at the weekend, when I'm supposed to be relaxing, I do all the washing, and wash the floors and then wash the car." "What about your husband?" asks her friend. "Oh him? I make him wash himself."

Teacher: "Do you ever have to help your mummy with the housework."
Little girl: "No. She usually seems to know what she's doing."

Why is that when dads do the hoovering and spot a big lump of fluff on the carpet they pick it up and look at it before putting it back down to hoover up?

Why is it that just when you get house looking clean and tidy the whole damn lot needs doing again a few months later?

Why do unexpected visitors only call when the place looks like a tip and you've got a mudpack on your face?

Dull women have immaculate homes.

Marrying is easy – it's housework that's hard.

"The obvious and fair solution to the housework problem is to let men do the housework for, say, the next six thousand years, to even things up. The trouble is that men, over the years, have developed an inflated notion of the importance of everything they do, so that before long they would turn housework into just as much of a charade as business is now. They would hire secretaries and buy computers and fly off to housework conferences in Bermuda, but they'd never clean anything."

Dave Barry

"Housework can't kill you, but why take a chance?"

Phyllis Diller

"Housekeeping is like being caught in a revolving door."

Marcelene Cox

"Housework, if you do it right, can kill you."

Erma Bombeck

A woman was putting together some self-assembly furniture while being watched by her friend's five year old son. When she found she needed a screwdriver, she asked the little boy if he would go and find one for her. "OK," said the little boy, "but do you want a 'daddy screwdriver' or a 'mummy screwdriver'." The woman wasn't sure what he meant but decided to opt for the "mummy screwdriver". The little boy came back a couple of few moments later and handed the woman a butter knife.

A mother and son were doing dishes while the father and daughter were watching TV in the living room. Suddenly, there was a loud crash of breaking plates, then complete silence. The daughter looked at her father and said confidently, "Mummy must have done it!" "How can you tell?" asked the dad. "She didn't say anything," said the daughter.

I thank the Lord I no longer have to go to work. I just get out of bed in the morning, and there it is – all around me.

"Housework is a treadmill from futility to oblivion with stop-offs at tedium and counter-productivity."

Erma Bombeck

"I buried a lot of my ironing in the back yard."

Phyllis Diller

"I hate housework. You make the beds, you wash the dishes and six months later you have to start all over again."

Joan Rivers

"Working mothers are the backbone of the third half of the economy."

Glenda Jackson

"I make no secret of the fact that I would rather lie on a sofa than sweep beneath it. But you have to be efficient if you're going to be lazy."

Shirley Conran

"If your house is really a mess and a stranger comes to the door, greet him with, 'Who could have done this? We have no enemies.'"

Phyllis Diller

"Love is the thing that enables a woman to sing while she mops up the floor after her husband has walked across it in his barn boots."

Hoosier Farmer

"My husband and I have figured out a really good system about the housework: neither one of us does it."

Dottie Archibald

"I try to take one day at a time, but sometimes several days attack me at once."

Jennifer Unlimited

My idea of housework is to sweep the room with a glance.

Betty's mother was visiting her daughter and son-in-law Bill. Bill came home from work and found six vacuum cleaner salesmen outside his house. He dashed in and said, "Mum, there are six men outside who all claim they have an appointment for a vacuum cleaner demonstration!" "That's right," the mother-in-law replied. "Now you just show them all to different rooms and let them start demonstrating."

"I'm 18 years behind in my ironing. There's no use doing it now, it doesn't fit anybody I know."

Phyllis Diller

"People can say what they like about the eternal verities, love and truth and so on, but nothing's as eternal as the dishes."

Margaret Mahy

"The worst thing about work in the house or home is that whatever you do it is destroyed, laid waste or eaten within 24 hours."

Lady Hasluck

"There is no need to do any housework at all. After the first four years the dirt doesn't get any worse."

Quentin Crisp

"A vacation frequently means that the family goes away for a rest, accompanied by mother, who sees that the others get it."

Marcelene Cox

"I don't know why no one ever thought to paste a label on the toilet-tissue spindle giving 1-2-3 directions for replacing the tissue on it. Then everyone in the house would know what Mama knows."

Erma Bombeck

Signs For Mum's Kitchen:

So this isn't Home Sweet Home... Adjust!

No, as you may have noticed, Nigella, Kim and Aggie, and Anthea Turner don't live here!

Ring bell for maid service. If no answer, do it yourself!

I clean this house every other day. Unfortunately today is the other day.

I would cook dinner but I can't find the tin opener!

My house was clean last week, too bad you missed it!

I came, I saw, I decided to order a takeaway.

If you don't like my standards of cooking... lower your standards.

Although you'll find our house a mess, Come in, sit down, converse. It doesn't always look like this: Some days it's even worse.

A messy kitchen is a happy kitchen, which means this kitchen must be delirious.

A balanced diet is a biscuit in each hand!

Blessed are they who can laugh at themselves for they shall never cease to be amused.

Countless number of people have eaten in this kitchen and gone on to lead normal lives.

My next house will have no kitchen... just vending machines.

I'd live life in the fast lane, but I am married to a speed bump.

Mum's Impossible Role Models

Mum's own mum
She of the perfect baking, darning and nursing skills.

Mary Poppins
Spoonful of sugar or not, my kids ain't taking medicine without a fight.
Those city superwomen who bring up four children and manage to run a multinational company in between times – though funnily enough, they never mention the legions of nannies, cooks, chauffeurs and au-pairs who help out just a little bit.

The mum in the *Famous Five* books
Somehow those kids in the old Enid Blyton stories managed to stay clean, clothed, and fed with something (all washed down with "lashings of ginger beer") with Mum staying firmly out of the picture. Oh, and they usually managed to arrest and turn in a few international jewel thieves too. Mrs Famous Five would of course be locked up nowadays for allowing her children to disappear for days at a time and fraternise with criminals.

The mythical mum
Deep in every woman's subconscious is an ideal of the perfect mother – probably some sort of impossible mixture of all the above. She is the one you are constantly trying, but failing, to emulate. She is a perfect cook, a perfect mentor, a perfect provider, and makes you perfectly sick. Whatever you do you will never live up to this fictitious perfect mother, so why not find a role model that you can top every time? Imagine the sort of mum

who microwaves every meal, lets the ironing pile up for weeks, lets the kids watch all sorts of rubbish on TV and is forever slobbing around in track suit bottoms with a glass of wine in hand. What do you mean it sounds just like you?

Nigella and co.

Those female celebrity cooks don't even have the one plus-point that their male counterparts do – i.e. they may be fanciable. There they are, in their perfect kitchens, with no toddlers running in and out or husbands nicking the cook's wine or the phone going every two minutes, knocking up fabulous concoctions with the unseen aid of helpers, gophers and endless retakes. Oh, if only real life were like that!

Celebrity mums

They appear in glossy magazines, coiffeured, impeccably made up and airbrushed with a rosy-cheeked bairn who looks like they've never cried or filled a nappy in their little life.

Mum's mother-in-law

Let's face it, your apple pie will never be as good as the semi-mythical homemade delight that your husband's mum served up to him when he was two years old, so don't try to compete; do your own delectable dishes. The chances are that your mother-in-law doesn't even know what the terms "goujon", "drizzled", or "rocket" mean, let alone attempt to incorporate them into her own cookery.

Sally Webster from *Coronation Street*

She seems to have got away with feeding her children on a constant diet of baked beans for 18 years and yet still hasn't been hauled in by Social Services

Royal mums

Every so often one of the extended royal family will produce yet another baby that will be spotted in celebrity magazines and tabloids. And however normal the mothers make their lives sound in the accompanying feature, you just have this sneaking feeling that they are probably not shopping at Primark and Lidl, or worrying too much about whether their lottery numbers are going to come up.

You Know You're A Mum When...

- Your kid throws up and you catch it.
- Someone else's kid throws up at a party. You keep eating.
- You find yourself cutting your husband's sandwiches into cute shapes.
- You can't bear to give away baby clothes – it's so final.
- You hear your mother's voice coming out of your mouth when you say, "NOT in your good clothes!"
- You stop criticizing the way your mother raised you.
- You donate to charities in the hope that your child won't get that disease.
- You hire a babysitter because you haven't been out with your husband in ages, then spend half the night checking on the kids.
- You use your own saliva to clean your child's face.
- You say at least once a day, "I'm not cut out for this job", but you know you wouldn't trade it for anything.
- Your feet stick to the kitchen floor... and you don't care.
- When the kids are fighting, you threaten to lock them in a room together and not let them out until someone is bleeding.
- You can't find your cordless phone, so you ask a friend to call you, and run around the house madly, following the sound until you locate the phone downstairs in the laundry basket.

- You spend an entire week wearing tracksuit bottoms.
- Your idea of a good day is making it through without a child leaking bodily fluids on you.
- Iced lollies have become a food staple.
- Your favourite television show is a cartoon.
- Your kids make jokes about flatulence, burping, pooping, etc. and you think it's funny.

Helpful Housework Hints For Mums

It's time to clean out the fridge when something closes the door from the inside.

If it walks out of your fridge, let it go!

The best hoover for a post-dinner clean up is the dog.

Never cook fried chicken in the nude.

If men were supposed to hang clothes up, there would be more door knobs.

Thou shalt not weigh more than thy refrigerator.

Simplify... hire a maid.

Cobwebs artfully draped over lampshades reduce the glare from the bulb, thereby creating a romantic atmosphere. If your husband points out that the light fixtures need dusting, simply look affronted and exclaim, "What? And spoil the mood?"

When writing your name in the dust on the table, omit the date.

If dust is REALLY out of control, simply place a showy urn on the coffee table and insist that "THIS is where Grandma wanted us to scatter her ashes..."

Ways Kids Can Drive Mums Mad

In the kitchen

They see you taking a chicken out of the oven two minutes before dinnertime and still ask what's for dinner.

Their idea of helping to unpack the shopping is to unpack the entire contents of a kilo bag of sugar on the kitchen floor.

No matter what other play areas are available to them around the house, they find the kitchen floor the absolute favourite location for cluttering with dolls, teddies, cars and other assorted objects that you are likely to trip over as you are transferring something extremely hot from the oven to the worktop.

In the garden

You can buy all the swings, slides, balls, bats and racquets you want, but they still much prefer to play with good old-fashioned mud.

After you have spent half an hour filling the paddling pool, elbow-testing it to the perfect temperature and covering the kids in factor 500 sun block, the little so and so's will then decide that on balance they'd rather watch TV.

Their idea of a nice surprise for Mum is to present her with a lovely bouquet of flowers – freshly picked from her own carefully tended flowerbeds.

In the car

They start to say they're starving before you even get to the end of your road.

When you pacify them with a few treats secreted in the glove compartment for such emergencies they then start on the "are we there yet?" routine.

The only time they finally drop off to sleep and give you a break is when you've arrived at your destination, and then you couldn't budge them from the car with dynamite.

In a restaurant

They say they don't like every single item on the menu which you have patiently read out to them one by one and then ask for the very item you suggested in the first place.

They suddenly find the area underneath the restaurant table infinitely more interesting than the bit on top where the food goes.

You can guarantee that the moment your long awaited meal is brought to your table one of your children will urgently need to go to the lavatory.

The Laws Of Household Physics

Ever notice that the laws of household physics are every bit as real as every other law in the universe? Here are a few examples:

A child's eagerness to assist in any project varies in inverse proportion to the ability to actually do the work involved.

Leftovers always expand to fill all available containers plus one.

A newly washed window gathers dirt at double the speed of an unwashed window.

The availability of a ballpoint pen is inversely proportional to how badly it is needed.

The same clutter that will fill a one-car garage will fill a two-car garage.

Three children plus two cookies equals a fight.

The potential for disaster is in direct proportion to the number of TV remote controls divided by the number of viewers.

The number of doors left open varies inversely with the outdoor temperature.

The capacity of any hot water heater is equal to one and one-half sibling showers.

What goes up must come down, except for bubble gum, kites and slightly used Rice Krispies.

Place two children in a room full of toys and they will both want to play with the same toy.

How To Avoid Ironing

Don't wash anything!

Pretend you're trying to save the planet by not wasting energy on ironing – your green-brainwashed children will surely approve.

Buy lots of clothes made from linen, crinkly fabric, or with folds and ruches etc which simply do not need ironing.

Put freshly-washed clothes under the cushions of the sofa. All those bottoms will soon have the clothes freshly pressed.

Take the fuse out of the iron and claim that it's broken down (again).

Ask Dad how he'd feel about having a nice young au pair to help out around the house.

Convince everyone that you're a born-again hippy and that ironing is just like such a bourgeois concept, man.

Use the logical argument that it's hardly worth as it as the clothes will be back in the wash in a couple of days anyway.

Mum's Rules Of The House

No institution can properly function without rules, and the home is no exception. Most of the time these rules are unwritten, but somehow tacitly understood by all members of the family. However, just to avoid confusion, here are some of the more common ones:

Arguments

Mum has the combined powers of the United Nations Secretary General and the head of ACAS as well as the wisdom of Solomon. Her decision is final.

Backchat

Backchat covers answering mother back, being cheeky, being rude, mumbling under your breath or even looking at her the wrong way. In extreme cases it will also cover thinking about being cheeky, being rude, mumbling under your breath or looking at her the wrong way. Don't forget: mums know what you're thinking even before you know what you are thinking.

Bathroom

The bathroom is one of mother's domains that the rest of the family have privileged access to. Bath toys are tolerated a) if they are not jammed up taps, b) left on floor so Mum stabs her foot on getting out of the bath, c) put on radiator so they melt gooey yellow plastic over it. Teenagers are allowed in bathroom on condition that they a) don't take over the entire bathroom cabinet with their toiletries, b) stain the sink with hair dye, c) keep each visit to a maximum of three days.

Bedtime

Bedtime is not negotiable. Bedtime is bedtime. Bedtime is not the equivalent of last orders at the pub meaning there is just time to ask for one last drink and have an extra few minutes watching TV.

Childrens' parties

The party bag was not invented so kids had something to be sick in on the way home, so party food will not consist entirely of E numbers and fizzy pop. Games will not include "pin the tail on the family pet", "trash the house" or "101 alternative places to put food apart from in mouth." Contents of party bag will not be worth more than a couple of quid a head. Mum will not enter into any keeping up with the Mrs Joneses in this area of child rearing. Birthday cake candles can only be extinguished by blowing, not by water pistols, garden hoses or fire extinguishers.

Clothes

There are only three places where clothes should be seen – on the body, in the wardrobe or in the washing. Places such as the end of the bed, on the floor or hanging over the banisters do not count, however neatly clothes have been deposited.

Dads

Dads have dual roles. Most of the time they are big, sulky kids with stubble and long trousers who are subject to all the rules of the house, then at some inexplicable point they suddenly transform into supreme beings who can mete out punishment, make ultimate decisions and pay for everything. This transformation from one personality to the other is entirely in the gift of Mum.

Food

Children are not meant to be a grazing species. Food is to be eaten at the table or not at all. Whoever invented the term TV dinner should be shot (just after cleaning all the crumbs off my living room floor).

Note: The fridge is Mother's exclusive domain. Even Father is only allowed special access when on catering duties.

Going out

When Mother asks where you are going, the answer she is looking for is not "out." She already knows you are going out because you have your coat on and are opening the front door. When Mother asks where you are going what she really wants to know is where precisely you are going, who with, an assurance that you won't be doing anything immoral, illegal, or embarrassing to her and that you will be home again before you turn 18. She will want to know the exact time you will be home, the state you will be in and have an assurance that you will leave your mobile phone switched on at all times. If any of the above rules are broken she will embarrass you severely by phoning all your friends' parents, the police and possibly MI5 to ascertain your whereabouts five minutes after the time you have said you will be home.

Junk

People think "decluttering" is a new concept. It isn't. Mums have been doing it since dads first had the cave strewn with animal bones and skins and other stuff he hadn't quite got round to finishing with. "Junk" will be defined by mum to mean "anything which has ceased to be useful around the house" – so, watch out, that could include you Dad. Mum will tolerate junk only for so long, then without so much as a two-minute warning, out will come the vacuum cleaner, the Marigolds, the dusters and various household cleaners in bottles shaped like guns, and the blitz will begin. At the end of it anything which hasn't been cleaned to within an inch of its life will be dumped, recycled, given away, thrown away or burned. You have been warned.

Kitchen

This is Mum's fiefdom where she has absolute control and absolute power. Even Dad has only limited access. It is full of extremely dangerous things: cookers, toasters, knives, etc. – not to mention Mum herself. Enter it at your peril, especially when Mum is in the middle of cooking.

Laundry

The deal is this: Mum will wash, iron and fold clothes or put onto hangers; the rest of the family simply have to put dirty washing in laundry basket. Mother will not know that you have chosen to put your dirty clothes under the bed until they begin to smell bad. Before putting clothes into washing basket remove tissues and other pieces of paper which will disintegrate into a million tiny pieces and make Mum's favourite black top look like it's just been dragged through a snow globe.

Living room

Perhaps it should be renamed the "existing room". "Living" implies an element of earthy abandon which Mum simply will not tolerate. This room will be kept looking spick and span at all times in the unlikely event that someone with a cleaner and tidier living room will come to visit. Cushions shall be permanently plumped, curtains neatly drawn and tied back, DVDs judiciously filed, and whole square yards of floor empty of junk to facilitate unencumbered walking. Enjoy!

Mealtimes

There is one mealtime for all the family. Everyone must arrive at the table simultaneously with hands washed. Mother will not listen to "I'll just finish watching this", or "I'll just finish doing that" before family members deign to arrive for a meal that has been slaved over for an hour and a half.

Sleep

When Mum is asleep, children must be asleep. When children are asleep Mum can get on with something. In extreme circumstances she may even enjoy herself.

Teenage parties

Parties are planned, not impromptu affairs that automatically happen when more than two teenagers bring a bottle of cider home. Parties must never happen when parents are away on holiday.

Table manners

In polite circles it is considered bad manners to use your dinner plate as a landing strip for your model aeroplane, to feed your favourite teddy bear with custard or to send text messages throughout dinner. All this is doubly so if you happen to be the father of the house.

Television

Now that "children's hour" lasts all day, Mum is allowed exclusive use of the TV from 7pm onwards. Children creep downstairs while Mum's watching her programmes at their peril.

Toys

Toys are to be kept in children's bedrooms. Any toys found on the stairs/in the kitchen/down the back of the radiator will be sent immediately to the nearest charity shop.

Washing

Washing hands is allowed without direct instructions from Mum. Washing in the bath is compulsory and not an irritating distraction from the serious business of playing with boats, submarines and ducks. Mum's favourite bubble bath is a dangerous substance. If touched by children, Mum will explode!

Signs That You Could Be A Frustrated Mother

Your children know how to read HTML code but can't operate a vacuum cleaner.

Your children tell you that you said "yes" and you don't even remember the question.

You go to the grocery store and find yourself having a good time.

Your husband asks how your day went and you rate it on a scale of 1-10 based on the number of times you repeated the phrase "stop that!" or "no!"

You can't remember the last time you didn't have to share your drink.

You mistakenly tell the kids it's "sanity" time when you meant to say "bed" time.

The laundry seems to have taken on an evil nature and you begin to feel that it's out to get you.

You dread hearing the phone ring because it's a sure sign there's about to be trouble amongst the children.

You go to sleep with "I'm bored" or "I'm hungry" still ringing in your ears.

You Know You're A Mum When...

You're up each night until 10pm vacuuming, dusting, wiping, washing, drying, loading, unloading, shopping, cooking, driving, flushing, ironing, sweeping, picking up, changing sheets, changing diapers, bathing, helping with homework, paying bills, budgeting, clipping coupons, folding clothes, putting to bed, dragging out of bed, brushing, chasing, buckling, feeding (them, not you), PLUS swinging, playing baseball, bike riding, pushing trucks, cuddling dolls, roller balding, basketball, football, catch, bubbles, sprinklers, slides, nature walks, colouring, crafts, jumping rope, PLUS raking, trimming, planting, edging, mowing, gardening, painting, and walking the dog. You get up at 5.30pm and you have no time to eat, sleep, drink or go to the bathroom, and yet you still managed to gain ten pounds.

In your bathroom there is toothpaste on the light fixtures, water all over the floor, a dog drinking out of the toilet and body hair forming a union to protest over unsafe working conditions.

You use your sunglasses instead of a hair clip to keep your hair out of your eyes. You no longer carry cash in your wallet, just lots of Band-Aids. You have 999 saved in your speed dial. You get excited at the sight of heavy farm machinery (especially when it is bright yellow and makes lots and lots of noise). You find yourself singing "Wheels on the Bus" in the shower. You know where every toilet is located in every shop you ever visit.

How To Avoid Washing Clothes

Always dress the children in black. OK, they'll look like automatons from *The Village of the Damned*, but the clothes will only need washing once every couple of weeks.

When the kids go through that stage of wanting to wear the same clothes again and again until they fall apart, don't argue. Any comments you get can be blamed on the children.

Take clothes back to the shop and exchange them after each wearing

The logical extension of disposable nappies is disposable clothing – invent your own range!

Buy everything "dry-clean only".

Tell the family you're all going nudist.

Take the kids to the nearest stream and let them learn how it was done in the "olden days" for their history project.

Things Mums Don't Appreciate Hearing From Dads

So, what have you been doing all day while I've been hard at work?

Damn it! They're forcing me to go on another one of these boring corporate golf trips.

The kids would never try that on with me.

How can a week's groceries be more than £50?

You should have just bought it for them.

You bought them what? You paid how much for it?

What do you need a new dress for? You never go anywhere.

Oooh dear. These client lunches really take it out of you.

More money? What for?

But I took them to the park last week.

Still, once you've packed them off to school you can put your feet up until it's time to collect them can't you?

It's not a father's role to help round the house.

Yes, you're the one who goes out to work and earns the money while I stay at home all day, but I still say it's not a father's role to help round the house.

Don't look at me. You were the one who wanted kids.

Oh, while you dozed off, I let the kids trim your hair for you.

Mum's Main Enemies In Life

Perfect Mums

There is nothing more infuriating for a mother struggling through another day's twin-fronted battle against the world and her children than to encounter one of those Perfect Mums.

There are three main problems with these people. Firstly that they are a perfect mum, secondly they know they are a perfect mum, and thirdly they are going to damn well make sure everyone else knows they are a Perfect Mum as well.

Being a Perfect Mum is not just a way of life for these people, it's a permanent demonstration to the rest of us lesser mortals of what we're doing wrong.

They have perfect children who are always perfectly behaved. There is no crisis they are not immediately equipped to deal with and life is all one great jolly game-cum-learning experience for them and their children.

There's nothing you can do though. These Perfect Mothers and their families have clearly all been created in a laboratory somewhere. The best you can hope for is that they will one day stand too close to a radiator and begin to melt.

School teachers

At least, the ones who probably don't have children of their own but hint that you are not doing your job properly and you have failed as a parent by putting the wrong stuff in the lunchboxes, not doing enough homework with the kids, and by taking them on holiday during school term.

Rubbish Mums

Curiously although Perfect Mums are really annoying, so are mums who have clearly no idea what they're doing at all. You'd think there would be some sense of superiority to be gleaned from the sight of mothers who have failed to develop the first idea of how to talk to, deal with and feed their children and are yelling and swearing at their offspring while attempting to stuff their mouths with a large sack of fried, bright orange E-numbers.

Even more frustratingly, these people are probably looking at us and hating us because they think we're Perfect Mothers.

Mums in TV adverts

These are even worse than Perfect Mums, because they're Perfect Mums as designed by people in the advertising industry. They're always gorgeous, beautifully attired and accompanied by husbands who are hunky, permanently good humoured but ever so slightly dim (well, they got one out of three right).

The mums in these adverts are very rarely depicted with children who have been possessed by Satan, who are screaming, "I hate yoooouuu!" and who then attack them with a sharpened turkey twizzler.

Don't forget though these people only have to pretend to be mums for the few seconds they are filmed for these adverts. If that was the length of time the rest of us had to be mums for each day, we'd all look perfect too.

Child experts

It's bad enough being lectured by smarty-pants child psychologists, nutritionists and other so-called experts, but when you're constantly reading the child-rearing advice of dotty celebrity mums in magazines who have armies of nannies, cleaners, cooks and gardeners, it does get your dander up

Other people's kids

They're either the perfect children you never had and make you feel inadequate as a mother, or they're the little sods who run wild in your house and wreck everything. In some extreme cases they're a detestable mixture of the two: hyperactive savants with behavioural problems – aarrghh!

Hairstyle Options For Mums

The Croydon Facelift – pulled back in a ponytail so tight it not only irons out your wrinkles, you get a nose-job and a permanent grin at the same time.

The Two-tone – these days you've neither got the time nor the money to go the hairdresser's regularly to have your roots done so you pretend it's actually a cool new style all by itself.

The Sigourney Weaver – a completely shaven head with minimal maintenance that leaves plenty of time for all those mum chores.

The Busy Beehive – However big your handbag, there's never enough room to store all the baby and child paraphernalia you have to cart around everywhere, so this is a handy additional storage space – and it's the height of fashion! (Well, 30 years ago anyway).

The Pink Punk Spiky Hairdo – Ok you will look a bit of a freak, but you probably will not be asked to man the cake stall at the Summer Fair or help out when the children go on a school outing or any of those other things mums get roped into, as you will frighten the children.

The Phil Spector fright wig – with 1001 other things to do in the morning before school it's not easy to find time to do much with your hair so invest in a selection of cheap but witty wigs as Phil Spector has done, and it doesn't matter what your real hair looks like.

Top Tips For Mums To Get Their Kids Helping Them Round The House

Lead by example – demonstrate to your kids how to do the chores round the house by letting them watch while you do them.

Of course if you follow this top tip you may find 18 years or more pass by without them ever quite picking up the methods you are trying to impart. Then they may leave and set up their own homes to which you may be invited to come and demonstrate for them how they should clean and tidy in this new environment. Perhaps another 18 years or so of demonstration will be required.

Make cleaning fun – Put on some music and dance around while you mop and scrub. Because cleaning is fun isn't it? Just look at those people who have to clean offices and other establishments for a living. They look like they're having more fun than anyone else in history of the world, don't they?

Make a big chore chart – This will be big colourful poster showing the different jobs that need doing round the house and which member of the family has to do them this week. Of course making the chore chart in the first place is itself yet another household chore that you'll probably end up having to do. On the other hand if you make a chart big enough you can then use it to place over and hide any piles of rubbish in the house that haven't been cleaned up. You may also find after a few weeks you have a massive chore chart with hundreds of jobs listed and the name "Mummy" in every single box alongside them.

Tell them that under no circumstances are they allowed to help. This will then make the jobs seem like the ultimate in unattainable desirability which must be achieved as soon as possible.

Get your kids to help wash the dishes – this idea cannot fail can it? Either the kids will clean the dishes for you or you will end up with no dishes intact and which therefore never need to be cleaned again.

Tell them that you have a contagious disease and touching anything they eat or eat off will kill them

Get kids to help prepare foods (bearing in mind their age) – by age ten, it is said children should be able to prepare a simple meal on their own, such as pasta with a bottled sauce. Then, once they've managed to do this, get them to teach you how to do this recipe as well. It sounds like it might come in handy!

Or if all else fails there's the old faithful: simply tell your kids that your will stipulates that all of your secretly accrued millions will go to your most loving and dutiful child

Things Mums Will Say To Each Other To Wind One Another Up

Oh these school fees are horrendous aren't they? Oh, I'm sorry, I forgot, your children are at state school aren't they?

Of course my little Jemima doesn't need extra coaching.

I think feeding them anything other than organic is tantamount to child abuse really.

Oh this is your little runaround while your husband uses the main car is it? Oh, he goes by train...?

It's so annoying when the nanny doesn't get on with the cleaner isn't it? Oh, you haven't got one?

I'd love to have a little part-time job like you but we're paying the top rate of tax already so it just wouldn't be worth it.

I don't need to sew nametags into my children's clothes because I know no one else at the school can afford those kind of designer labels.

Have you ever thought about plastic surgery? Not that you need it of course.

So, have you had the baby yet or not?

Things Mums Can Say To Perfect Mothers To Take The Wind Out Of Their Sails

Your child is very well behaved isn't he? Although of course if mine were that well behaved I'd be slightly worried they weren't quite normal.

Wow! You like to keep them in perfect control don't you? In fact – and please don't take this the wrong way – you remind me ever so slightly of Hitler...

Of course the better behaved they are now, the greater and more devastating the rebellion in years to come.

You've got your children perfectly behaved haven't you? And of course they will be able to develop their own inner resources and personalities when they ultimately escape you and swear never to see you again.

Do you know, there's times I wish my children were as terrified of me as yours clearly are of you.

Wow! Your little boy has already become a member of Mensa? He's just like Jimmy Savile!

Your little girl's having private tuition, is she? You must be terribly worried about how badly she's been falling behind at school?

Your little boy's always so well turned out and with such perfect manners – do you ever think he might be gay?

Emergency Medical Advice As Given By Children

Before giving a blood transfusion, find out if the blood is affirmative or negative.

To remove a speck of dust from the eye: pull the eye down over the nose.

For a nosebleed: put the nose much lower then the body until the heart stops.

For drowning: climb on top of the person and move up and down to make artificial perspiration.

For fainting: rub the person's chest or, if a lady, rub her arm above the hand instead. Or put the head between the knees of the nearest medical doctor.

For dog bite: put the dog away for several days. If he has not recovered, then kill it.

For asphyxiation: apply artificial respiration until the patient is dead.

For head cold: use an agonizer to spray the nose until it drops in your throat.

For fractures: to see if the limb is broken, wiggle it gently back and forth.

Things You'll Never Hear A Mum Say...

How on earth can you see the TV sitting so far back?

Yeah, I used to skip school a lot, too.

Just leave all the lights on... it makes the house look more cheery.

Let me smell that shirt... Yes, that'll be good for another week.

Go ahead and keep that stray dog, darling. I'll be glad to feed and walk him every day.

The curfew is just a general time to shoot for. It's not like I'm running a prison around here.

I don't have a tissue with me... So just pick your nose a bit then use your sleeve.

Don't bother wearing a jacket – the wind-chill is bound to improve.

Be good and for your birthday I'll buy you a motorcycle!

I think a cluttered bedroom is a sign of creativity.

Could you turn the music up louder so I can enjoy it, too?

Run and bring me the scissors! Go on! Quick! Hurry!

I'll tell you what, just turn those dirty underpants inside out. No one will ever know.

Well, if Tom's mum says it's OK, that's good enough for me.

My meeting won't be over till late tonight. You kids don't mind if we skip dinner do you?

Of course you should walk to school and back now you're a big boy of four years old. What's the big deal about having to cross a few main roads?

Things Mums Definitely Don't Want To Hear Their Kids Say

Wow! Come and see the colour I've made the baby go!

Is it true you're a professional prize fighter, Mum? 'Cause Darren's mum said you're a right slapper.

When do I get a step-mum? Everyone else at school has got one.

How do you fix a cat's tail back on?

Is it true you're doing a cleaning job on the side, Mum? 'Cause Darren's mum said you're a right scrubber.

Can we get an automatic car? I hate driving with gears.

I've made you a sandwich from things I found outside. I know you'll eat it all up because you love me.

I've managed to get all the paint off one half of the car. Please can I have another Brillo pad?

Is it true you've had some kind of pioneering transplant surgery using organs taken from other animals, Mum? 'Cause Darren's mum said you're a bit of a dog, a bit of a cow and a bit of an old trout.

For show and tell at school today, I took that funny photograph Daddy took of you in the bath.

Needless Additional Burdens In A Mum's Life

Having to feed and look after a selection of hamsters, guinea pigs, rats, stick insects and cats and dogs as well as children.

Having to check every packet of food for E-numbers, additives, fat content, cholesterol, nuts and 1001 other toxic baddies.

Having to keep up with the Mrs Joneses not just with house, car, hair, make-up and clothes, but also kids' clothes, lunchbox contents and holiday destinations too.

Not just worrying about the age children start crossing the road on their own or dating, but also at what age they can have heelies, mobile phones, and their own Facebook pages.

Peer group pressure from other mums to do yoga, pilates, colonic irrigation and body waxing as well as the usual coffee mornings, etc.

Having to search the Internet every night for information needed to complete homework.

Having to learn all the new slang so you can understand whet the hell your children are saying to you.

Having to accompany them on trick or treat, penny for the guy, carol singing and other nocturnal expeditions.

Getting roped into various "raising money for the school" activities when you thought you were already doing that through the tax system.

Family Stress Test

How to score: 0 if the statement is never true, 1 if it is rarely true, 2 if it is sometimes true, and 3 if it is always true.

1. Conversations often begin with "Put the gun down, and then "we can talk."
2. The school headmaster has your number on speed-dial.
3. Your cat is on Valium.
4. People have trouble understanding your kids, because they learned to speak through clenched teeth.
5. You are trying to get your four-year-old to switch to decaf.
6. The number of jobs held down by family members exceeds the number of people in the family.
7. No one has time to wait for microwave TV dinners.
8. "Family meetings" are often mediated by law enforcement officials.
9. You have to check your kid's day-planner to see if he can take out the rubbish.
10. You get bulk purchase rates on your regular supply of caffeine pills.

How you rate:
30: A perfect score. Welcome to the neighbourhood!
20-29: You are doing reasonably well, but still have too little going on in your life. Crank it up.
10-19: You have mastered some of the aspects of the stress-filled life, but still have a long way to go. Have you considered a parallel career path?
0-9: Enjoying all that extra time? What do you do anyway?

Thank God They're At School All Day Now...

Their first day of school is that bittersweet moment when you know you won't be sharing marmite soldiers in front of *Postman Pat* with your tiny tot ever again, but hurrah, your adult life will resume normal service! Well, perhaps not quite normal service, because all though you won't be at the beck and call of a four-year-old's insatiable demands throughout the day, you will now be a sort of unpaid member of the school staff, providing not only school clothing, games kit, lunches, and all the rest, but you will be expected to come up with brilliant, innovative and home-made contributions to cake sales, harvest festivals, halloween parties and mufti days, as well as celebrations for Easter, Christmas, Eid, Diwali, Hanukkah, and religious festivals you have never even dreamt of before. On top of that you will need to attend sports days, carol services, Christingles, firework nights, plays, concerts, PTA meetings, coffee mornings, open evenings, parents' quiz nights, barbecues, Summer fetes and 101 other events. And even when you get your child home there's reading time, homework, and sifting through the sheaf of notices from teachers, head teachers, school secretaries and PTA chairs. *Postman Pat*, we're missing you already!

Note to new teacher from a mum: "If you promise not to believe everything my child says happens at home, I'll promise not to believe everything he says happens at school."

On the first day of school, a first-year pupil hands his teacher a note from his mother which reads: "The opinions expressed by this child are not necessarily those of his parents."

A teacher gives her class a science lesson on magnetism. The next day she wants to see how much of the lesson the class has remembered. So she says, "I want you to write down the thing I'm thinking of. I'll give you a few clues. It's a word, it's six letters long, it begins with "m" and it picks things up. What is it?" Eighty per cent of the class write down "mother".

School days are the happiest of your life aren't they? Especially when you're a mum – they keep the kids out of your hair all day!

A little boy comes home from school one day and tells his mum his teacher asked if he had a younger brother or sister who might be coming to the school as well. "That's nice," says Mum. "So what did she say when you told her that you're an only child?" "She said, 'Thank God for that!'" says the little boy.

A little girl had just started school. After one week she came home and told her mum it was a complete waste of time. "Why's that?" asked her mum. "I can't read, I can't write and they won't let me talk!" said the little girl.

Mum calls up the stairs, "Come on Peter, it's time to get out of bed and go to school." "Don't want to go," moans Peter. "I hate school!" "Oh come on now, Peter," says his mum. "Give me two good reasons why you don't want to go." "Well," he says, "Firstly, all the children hate me, and secondly, their mums and dads hate me as well! Can you give me two good reasons why I should go to school?" "Yes," says his mum. "First, you're 47 years old, second, you're the headmaster."

"Mummy," says a little boy. "The boys at school say I've got a really huge enormous head." "Now don't you pay those boys any attention," says his mother. "There's nothing wrong with your head. Now go down to the shops for me and buy me a cabbages, six turnips, and ten pounds of spuds." "Yes, Mummy," says the little boy. "Shall I take the shopping bag?" "No," says his mum. "Just do what you usually do and stick them all in your balaclava."

On his first day at school little Jonathan has only been in the classroom for a few minutes when he suddenly realises he needs to go to the toilet. He asks the teacher for permission and she tells him to hurry along as she has some important things to explain to the new children. After ten minutes Jonathan comes back looking flustered. "All right now Jonathan?" asks the teacher. "No, miss. I couldn't find it," he replies. "Look," she says, scribbling on a piece of paper, "I've done you a little map, just follow this and it'll be easy to find." After another ten minutes Jonathan comes back looking more flustered and embarrassed. "I still can't find it," he says. "Brett," says the teacher to another boy, "you've been here a term, will you show Jonathan where it is?" So Brett takes him off down the corridor and brings him back after two or three minutes. "Did you find it this time?" asks the teacher. "Oh yes," says Brett, we found it eventually – he had his trousers on backwards."

On his first day at nursery school a little boy was told that if he needed to go the toilet he should hold up his hand. "How will that help?" asked the little boy.

"All kids are gifted; some just open their packages earlier than others."

Michael Carr

A Sunday school teacher asks her pupils where they think God lives. A small girl puts her hand up and says, "Miss, I think God lives in our bathroom." "In your bathroom?" says the teacher. "Why do you think he's in there?" "Because," says the girl, "every morning my daddy keeps banging on the bathroom door and shouting, 'God, are you still in there?'"

On the first day at school the children are sizing each other up and boasting in an attempt to make the best impression on their school mates. "I come from a one-parent family," says one little girl proudly. "Oh yeah? That's nothing," says a little boy. "Both my parents remarried after they got divorced. So I come from a four-parent family."

One teacher says to another, "I had a funny feeling little Sammy was having trouble at home." The second teacher asks, "Why?" The first explains, "When I asked him what he wanted to be when he grew up he said 'an orphan.'"

A school teacher is trying to stop her pupils using so much slang. When she meets her new class for the first time in September she begins by saying: "Now class, there are two words I simply will not tolerate in this class in written or spoken English. One of them is 'gross' and the other one is 'cool'" There is short silence, then one of the boys says, "Wow, so are you going to tell us what the two words are?"

A teacher asked his pupils during an English lesson, "Class, can anyone tell me, what do you call a person who keeps on talking when people are no longer interested?" From the back of the class a little boy's voice piped up, "A teacher!"

A schoolteacher has asked her class of five year olds to draw any picture of their choice. She walks around looking at all the children's drawings and notices that one little girl is drawing a picture of what seems to be a man. "Who's that?" asks the teacher, "Is it your daddy?" "No," replies the little girl, "it's God." "But no one knows what God looks like," says the teacher. "They will in a minute," says the little girl, still drawing.

A teacher stops a little boy running into school. "Hello," says the teacher. "You're new this term aren't you? What's your name?" "Reece," says the little boy. "Reece?" says the teacher. "Reece what?" The little boy looks blank. "Come on, boy!" says the teacher. "Don't you know your full name? What comes after Reece?" "Reece, stop it you little bugger?" suggests Reece.

A teacher asks little Johnny, "How is it possible for one person to make so many silly mistakes in a single day?" "I get up early," says Johnny.

A teacher is doing a spelling test with her class. She asks, "Who can the spell the word dynamite?" A little boy puts his hand up and spells out, "T – N – T!"

A school teacher was doing a lesson on slogans used in advertising. He asked the children in his class which company used the phrase "I'm lovin' it" and a lot of hands went up and the correct answer was given. Then he tried, "Finger lickin' good" and again hands went up and the children knew the right answer. "Right then," said the teacher, "which of you knows who uses the slogan 'Just do it!'" And a little boy put his hand up and said, "My mum!"

An English teacher says to her pupils, "I want each of you to imagine you've got a million pounds and to write an essay on what they think they would do if they had a million pounds. After 20 minutes she collects in the essays but is annoyed to find one of the boys has left his paper completely blank. "Alec!" yells the teacher, "you've done nothing at all!" "Yes, miss," says Alec. "Why not?" asks the teacher. "Because," says the boy, "if I had a million pounds, that's exactly what I'd do!"

Little Billie's teacher was asking the class about the alphabet. "So, Billie," she asked, "can you tell me what it is that comes after 'O'?" Little Billie thought for a moment and then said, "Yeah?"

One day at school a little boy is asked by his teacher, "What is the Fifth Commandment?" "Humour thy father and mother," he replies.

Lucy's class are learning about ethics as part of their humanities studies and the teacher gives them an example of a real-life situation. "A man is playing football with his little boy near a river," says the teacher, "and the boy accidentally kicks the ball in. The man wades in to retrieve it and then stumbles and because he can't swim, cannot get back to dry land. He flails in the deep water and shouts for help. Then his wife notices what has happened and races down to the bank. What did she do next?" Lucy puts her hand up and suggests, "Draw out all his money?"

During class, a chemistry teacher was demonstrating the properties of various acids. "Now I'm dropping this silver coin into this glass of acid," said the teacher. "Do you think it will dissolve?" "No, sir," a student called out. "Excellent!" beamed the teacher. "And can you can explain to the rest of the class why the silver coin won't dissolve." "Because if it would," said the student, "you wouldn't have dropped it in there."

A little boy asks his teacher, "Miss, would you punish me for something I haven't done?" "No, of course not," says the teacher. "Thank goodness for that," says the little boy. "Because I haven't done my homework."

"If there were no schools to take the children away from home part of the time, the insane asylum would be filled with mothers."

Edgar Watson Howe

A little girl is trying to do her maths homework and asks her mum, "Mum, can you help me find the lowest common denominator?" "Good grief," says mum, "Don't tell me they still haven't found that. They were looking for it when I was at school!"

Little James is doing his maths homework at the kitchen table while his mum looks on proudly. "Two plus two, the son of a bitch is four, three plus three, the son of a bitch is six, four plus four, the son of a bitch..." "Hey," says Mum, "what did you just you say? Who taught you to do your sums like that?" "Mrs Parkinson," says James. "My teacher." "Right!" says Mum, I'm going straight up to the school now to have a word with Mrs Parkinson. I think it's disgusting the way she's teaching children to speak!" When she gets there she furiously demands to know why the teacher has been teaching her little boy to do maths in this way. "No, no no," says Mrs Parkinson, "I told him: two plus two, the sum of which is four!"

A teacher asks one of her pupils, "Did your mummy and daddy help you with these homework problems?" "No," says the little boy, "I got them wrong all by myself!"

Teacher: "Jonathan, I think you've been copying – this story you've written about your pet budgie is almost exactly the same as your brother's story. And if it's not copying, how do you explain it?" Boy: "It's the same budgie, sir."

Mum receives Callum's spelling test results and they are absolutely appalling. "My goodness Callum, this is terrible. Why did you do so badly – you usually do quite well in these spelling tests?" "Yeah, I know, mum," says Callum. "But it was due to absence." "What do you mean? You weren't off school the day they had the spelling test," said mum. "No, I know I wasn't," says Callum, "but the boy who usually sits next to me was."

> **"When I was young, I was put in a school for retarded kids for two years before they realized I actually had a hearing loss. And they called ME slow!"**
>
> **Kathy Buckley**

Teacher: "Now class, who can tell me who knocked down the walls of Jericho?" Boy: "It wasn't me, miss."

Two little girls are discussing their new primary school teacher. "How old do you think she is?" asks the first. "I don't know," says the second little girl. "She looks quite old, doesn't she?" "We should try looking inside her knickers to find out," says the first. "How is that going to help us find out how old she is?" asks her friend. "It'll have it written inside," replies the first. "Mine say, 'six to seven years.'"

Because of the drugs problems in a certain area, the junior school was having a special day to educate children about the advantages of a drug-free society. All the parents were told in advance about the initiative, and when little Molly came home from school her mum asked her what she'd been taught about drugs. "Well Mum, I think our school is the best place to get them because they're free."

A little boy comes home from school and tells his mother he's been given a part in the school play. "Wonderful! What part is it?" replies his mother. The boy says, "I play the part of the husband." The mother scowls "That's terrible. Go back and tell the teacher you want a speaking part."

A group of school children had their picture taken for the school photograph and their teacher was trying to persuade them each to buy a copy of their group picture. "Just think how nice it will be," said the teacher, "to look at this picture when you are all grown up. You'll be able to look at it and say, 'There's Jennifer, she's a lawyer now,' or 'That's Michael. He's a doctor now.'" And a small voice at the back of the room joined in, "And look! There's the teacher. She's dead now."

At a school sports day, a mum was asked by her young son if she'd take part in some of the races. The mum said she would and asked him to tell her when they were ready to start. When it was time for the sack race, the little boy came bounding across the field shouting at the top of his voice, "Mummy! Hurry up! It's time for the old bag race and everyone's waiting for you."

Two little girls are talking in the school yard. "Can people predict the future with cards?" asks one. "My mother can," says the other. "Really?" says the first. "Yes," says her friend, "she took one look at my report card and told me exactly what was going to happen when my dad got home."

A junior school end of term concert is approaching and little Johnny is trying to think of what he can do in the show. His friend Mary is going to play a piano solo, his friend Tommy is going to recite a poem, but he can't think what he can do. Finally, his teacher is relieved to hear he has an act. Come the night of the concert, proud parents fill the school hall and watch delightedly as Mary, dressed in her prettiest frock, tinkles the ivories and Tommy, in his best suit, recites his poems. Last but not least comes little Johnny who steps up and announces, "Ladies and Gentlemen. My uncle owns a farm and every holiday I visit him there. Tonight, I would like to share with you my impression of some of the many sounds I hear on my uncle's farm. Here is the first... 'JOHNNY! GET OFF THAT F... LIPPING TRACTOR!'"

On a special teacher's day, a kindergarten teacher was receiving gifts from her pupils. The florist's son handed her a gift. She felt the wrapped up parcel, gave it a shake, held it over her head and said, "I bet I know what's in here – flowers!" "That's right!" said the boy, "but how did you know?" "Just a wild guess," she said. The next pupil was the sweet shop owner's daughter. The teacher held her gift overhead, shook it, and said, "I bet I can guess what it is – a box of sweeties!" "That's right! But how did you know?" asked the girl. "Just a lucky guess," said the teacher. The next gift was from the local off-licence owner's son. The teacher held the bag over her head and noticed that it was leaking. She touched a drop of the leakage with her finger and tasted it. "Is it wine?" she asked. "No," the boy replied. The teacher repeated the process, touching another drop of the leakage to her tongue. "Is it champagne?" she asked. "No," the boy replied. The teacher then said, "I give up, what is it?" The boy replied, "A puppy!"

Signs You May Have Put Your Child In The Wrong Primary School

Your child comes home without glasses claiming to have lost them in a game of "Lord of the Flies."

At picking-up time you hear a voice from his classroom saying, "OK, kids! Gather 'round the pentagram for sing-a-long time!"

The practice of "trapping and killing your lunch" was not mentioned in the school prospectus.

A leather-clad teacher announces that today's letters are S and M.

The classroom hamster is really just a wad of cotton from an aspirin bottle.

Potty training involves a lighter, a clip and rolling papers.

You find your child may not be able to say her ABC's, but she can re-sole your Nikes in 20 seconds flat.

Even the baby bottles have pierced nipples.

The teacher sends you home a note reading, "Your snot-nosed little bastard keeps getting into my tequila."

On the first day, the children are divided into "pimps" and "hos".

Advice From Kids On Romantic Issues

"Shake your hips and hope for the best."

Girl aged nine (On how you can make someone fall in love with you)

"My mother says to look for a man who is kind. That's what I'll do. I'll find somebody who's kinda tall and handsome."

Girl aged eight

"One of the people has freckles, and so he finds somebody else who has freckles too."

Boy aged six (on selecting a life partner)

"Eighty-four! Because at that age, you don't have to work anymore, and you can spend all your time loving each other in your bedroom."

Girl aged eight (on what was the best age at which to get married)

"No age is good to get married at. You got to be a fool to get married."

Boy aged six (on what's the best age at which to get married)

"It's better for girls to be single but not for boys. Boys need someone to clean up after them."

Girl aged nine (on marriage)

Well Known Proverbs Completed By School Kids

A primary school teacher in the USA did a test with her class on some well known proverbs. She gave the children the first half of the proverbs and asked them to finish the sayings off. The following are some of the results:

Better to be safe than... Punch a fifth grader.

Strike while the... Bug is close.

It's always darkest before... Daylight savings time.

Never underestimate the power of... Termites.

You can lead a horse to water but... How?

Don't bite the hand that... Looks dirty.

No news is... Impossible.

A miss is as good as a... Mr.

You can't teach an old dog... Maths.

If you lie down with dogs, you... Will stink in the morning.

Love all, trust... Me.

The pen is mightier than... The pigs.

An idle mind is... The best way to relax.

Where there is smoke, there's... Pollution.

Happy is the bride who... Gets all the presents.

A penny saved is... Not much.

Two is company, three's... The Musketeers.

None are so blind as... Stevie Wonder.

Children should be seen and not... Spanked or grounded.

If at first you don't succeed... Get new batteries.

You get out of something what you... See pictured on the box.

When the blind lead the blind... Get out of the way.

There is no fool like... Aunt Edie.

Laugh and the whole world laughs with you. Cry and... You have to blow your nose.

Different Approaches To Doing The School Run

The healthy walk – especially healthy for mum, who is carrying all the schoolbags, lunchboxes and sports kit.

The "ooh look, it might rain" drop-off in the car because Mum just can't face the walk.

The "I've got a new car and I want to show it off to the other mums" drop-off.

The "greener than thou" walk to prove a point to those gas-guzzling mums.

The snatch squad tactic – screech to a halt outside the gates with the 4x4 parked at a jaunty angle halfway across the road, race in and bundle the kids in and zoom off in a cloud of dust before you get caught up in the school run traffic jam.

Genuine Excuses Given By Mums For Keeping Their Kids Sick Off School

Carlos was absent yesterday because he was playing football. He was hurt in the growing part.

Excuse Roland from PE for a few days. Yesterday he fell out of tree and misplaced his hip.

My son is under a doctor's care and should not take PE today. Please execute him.

Please excuse Gloria from Jim today. She is administrating.

Please excuse Jennifer for missing school yesterday. We forgot to get the Sunday paper off the porch, and when we found it on Monday, we thought it was Sunday.

Please excuse Jimmy for being. It was his father's fault.

Please excuse Tommy for being absent yesterday. He had diarrhoea and his boots leak.

Sally won't be in school a week from Friday. We have to attend her funeral.

Please excuse Lisa for being absent. She was sick and I had her shot.

Dear School: Please ekscuse John being absent on Jan. 28, 29, 30, 31, 32, and also 33.

John has been absent because he had two teeth taken out of his face.

Megan could not come to school today because she has been bothered by very close veins.

Chris will not be in school 'cos he has an acre in his side.

Please excuse Ray Friday from school. He has very loose vowels.

Please excuse Pedro from being absent yesterday. He had (diahre) (dyrea)(direathe) the shits.

Irving was absent yesterday because he missed his bust.

I kept Billie home because she had to go Christmas shopping because I don't know what size she wear.

My daughter was absent yesterday because she was tired. She spent a weekend with the Marines.

Please excuse Jason for being absent yesterday. He had a cold and could not breed well.

Please excuse Mary for being absent yesterday. She was in bed with gramps.

Gloria was absent yesterday as she was having a gang over.

Please excuse Burma, she has been sick and under the doctor.

Maryann was absent December 11-16, because she had a fever, sore throat, headache and upset stomach. Her sister was also sick, fever and sore throat, her brother had a low grade fever and ached all over. I wasn't the best either, sore throat and fever. There must be something going around, her father even got hot last night.

Please excuse little Jimmy for not being in school yesterday. His father is gone and I could not get him ready because I was in bed with the doctor.

Please excuse Bob from school from Sep. 1 - Nov. 1, he had to attend a religious sacrificial giving ceremony on Indian grounds.

I didn't come to school yesterday because I was feeling like I was going to be sick, but thankfully I wasn't!

Please excuse my daughter for being late. Her broom won't start so I had to send it back to Salem for repairs!

I'm sorry but my babysitter flushed my homework down the toilet.

I'm sorry I can't come to school today because I have toemonia!

Tell-tale Signs You've Been Helping The Kids With Their Homework

Geography
Your kids talk about Peking instead of Beijing and all their temperatures are in Fahrenheit.

History
Your kids query whether the miner's strike is actually history as it only seems like last week.

English
All your kids' answers are spelt correctly.

Maths
Your kids' answer to the question that begins, "If Julie buys ten apples for ten pence and six oranges for 12 pence" is "At what supermarket is this supposed to have happened then?"

Information Technology
Your kids ask what a "download" is.

Physics
Your kids appear to know before the rest of the class that $E=MC^2$ is nothing to do with rave culture.

Chemistry
Your kids correctly choose in a multiple choice question that a chemical compound is not a place where they round up stray chemicals.

Messages From The Kids' School Mums Would Like To Receive

Your child has excelled.

Your child's exam results are fantastic.

Your child has been picked for the school team.

Your child has achieved record results in their end of year exams.

The other pupils have just elected your child head of year.

Thanks to efforts made by your child working entirely their own, the school has won a special award.

Your child has distinguished themselves in science.

We have decided to re-name the school in honour of your child.

Things You Probably Shouldn't Pack In Your Kids' Lunchboxes

Anything (like hard-boiled eggs) that they might be tempted to use as missiles.

Anything containing nuts, or that may contain nuts in case they share these with a friend whose mother will then sue you for millions.

Anything that's "good for them" because they won't eat it anyway.

Anything homemade. If it doesn't come in a packet – especially with a logo or a cartoon figure – they won't eat it.

Leftovers from last night's dinner. They'll tell the teacher who will call in social services and take you to court for child abuse.

Alcopops – apart from being bad for the children the teachers might be tempted to pinch them.

A completely healthy nutritionally balanced lunch with absolutely no treats – the other mums will hate you for it.

Little plastic knives and forks that can be used as offensive weapons by playground bullies or possibly to saw through the bars on the classroom windows prior to a mass break out.

Things Mums Learn At School

There is a subtle difference between looking like you haven't made any effort to look good at drop-off time and not actually making any effort to look good at drop-off time.

Children will behave much better at school than they do at home.

You will be judged by other mothers on all aspects of your and your child's appearance, possessions and general behaviour despite an outward display of girlie camaraderie.

To teachers, you are the enemy.

Don't let anyone know of any skills or abilities you possess that can be commandeered at the next fete/fair/bring and buy sale.

Never have any good ideas for fundraising, as you will be chosen to organise them before you can say School Fete.

The school is constantly teeming with bugs and germs and no one can escape!

That if you include school trips, after-school activities, sports fixtures, homework and all the rest, the school day is actually about 18 hours long!

Celebrity Mums

Madonna
Clearly not that much like a virgin then.

Charlotte Church
But will she still have "the voice of an angel" when she's woken up by the baby at 3am?

Sharon Osbourne
You'd think she'd have had her hands full enough with Ozzy, never mind having kids as well.

Posh Spice
Oh no! Just think! Only another few years and we're going to have a full set of Junior Spice Girls.

Jordan
Slight pause while we all make up our own breastfeeding jokes!

The Oxo mum
A great role model and Earth mother for generations. And she changes with the times too. Do you know you can now get vegetarian Oxo cubes? Presumably from an Ox that's not made of meat.

Marie Osmond
You'd think that working for all those years with little Jimmy would have put her off having kids of her own for life, but no, not a bit of it – she's got teenagers. Makes you feel old doesn't it?

Sharon Stone
It's nice to know that even sex symbols have to lose their figures and slob around in clothes that look like the marquees from one of their fabulous garden parties isn't it?

Britney Spears
Oops, she did it again!

Christina Aguilera
Was there some sort of subliminal message in her songs telling her to have children – "What A Girl Wants", "Come On Over baby", "Nobody Wants To Be Lonely"...?

Heidi Klum
If you're married to a Seal do you have babies or pups?

Geri Halliwell
This is the girl who helped to sing "2 Become 1" with the Spice Girls. She missed a golden opportunity to do a remake when she became pregnant: "1 becomes 2."

Queen Elizabeth II
The poor woman has had more grief with her kids than the average single mum on a rough housing estate, so count your blessings M'am!

Cherie Blair/Booth
A rare example of a Prime Minister's wife having a baby while her husband was in Downing Street. Certain European politicians were even more shocked that after many years of marriage a politician was actually still having sex with his own wife.

Lady Thatcher

Two kids. One got lost in the desert, one got found in the jungle. These are the sorts of things that happen when mums' backs are turned.

Andy Murray's mum

It must be strange when your mum is also your tennis coach – especially when you're a teenager. "You can't tell me what to do! Oh. I suppose you can actually."

Dennis the Menace's mum

Stood by and allowed her husband to beat her little boy with a slipper for the smallest of misdemeanours but for some reason none of the neighbours ever put in a call to social services.

Messages From The Kids' School Mums Wouldn't Like To Receive Quite So Much

Your child has been expelled.

Your child's exam results are fantastical.

Your child has been picked from a police line-up.

Your child has achieved record results in their end of year exams – but not in a good way.

The other pupils have all just signed a petition asking for your child to be removed from school.

Thanks to efforts made by your child working entirely on their own, this school has been placed on special measures.

Your child has blown up the school science block.

We have decided to re-name the school so it will no longer be associated in the public mind with your child.

Troublesome Children

"Troublesome kids" is probably a tautological statement like "useless men" or "police intelligence", but some kids are definitely more trouble than others. Thankfully, the most troublesome ones are usually other people's.

> **"Children today are tyrants. They contradict their parents, gobble their food, and tyrannize their teachers."**
>
> **Socrates (c 470 BC - 399 BC)**

A mother of three extremely troublesome little children was once asked whether or not she'd have children if she had the chance to do it all over again. She said, yes of course she would – "Just not the same ones."

A mum was overheard trying to deal with a noisy, unruly child. "Of course you're not adopted," she told the child, "if you were I'd have returned you long ago!"

A mum said to her little boy, "Will you behave?" And the little boy replied, "I'm being haive!"

Emily was a war baby. Every time they saw her, her parents started fighting.

Children can't win. If they're too noisy, they get punished and if they're too quiet, they get taken to the doctor's.

A six-year-old comes crying to his mother because his little sister pulled his hair. "Now don't be angry," says the mother. "Your sister's still very little. She doesn't realise that pulling hair hurts." The little boy goes back out. A minute later the mum hears the sound of screaming from the next room. Mum goes to investigate and finds the little girl now bawling her head off. Mum glances at the little boy who looks up at her and says cheerfully, "She knows now."

A harassed mother goes to the hospital A&E department and asked to speak to a consultant urgently. "Doctor, do you think a seven-year-old boy can perform an operation on himself, without anaesthetic, and remove his own appendix? "Don't be silly," says the consultant, "Of course he can't." The mother turns to the boy and says, "See, I told you! Now put it back at once!"

The reason why children have middle names: So they know when they're in REAL trouble.

A four-year-old little boy ran screaming out of the bathroom. His mummy asked him what the matter was and he explained that he'd just dropped his toothbrush into the toilet bowl. So the mum went into the bathroom, reached into the toilet bowl, fished out the toothbrush and threw it away in the rubbish bin. The little boy thought for a moment then went and got his mum's toothbrush. "We better get rid of this one as well then," he said. "Why's that?" asked his mum. "Well," he said, "I knocked this one into the toilet a couple of days ago."

> **"Experts say you should never hit your children in anger. When is a good time? When you're feeling festive?"**
>
> **Roseanne**

My mum was very good to me when I was young. She said she was going to get someone to take care of me – permanently. The only trouble was she said that the hit men were too expensive.

The summer holidays are the time of year when parents realise just how grossly underpaid teachers really are.

A little boy asks his mum if he is a gifted child. "Of course you are," says mum, "no one in their right mind would have paid for you, would they?"

The mum and dad of a really difficult little boy are at their wit's end to know what to do with the little tearaway. When it comes round to his birthday they discuss what to give him for a present that might help calm him down and behave a bit better. The mother says, "I know. Let's buy him a bicycle." "Well," says the father, "Maybe. But do you really think buying him a bicycle is going to improve his behaviour?" "Possibly not," says the mother, "but at least it will spread it over a wider area."

> **"As a child you never quite understood how your mum was able to know exactly what you were thinking... Sometimes Mum would know what you were thinking before the thought entered your head. 'Don't even think about punching your brother,' she would warn, before you had time to make a fist."**
>
> **Linda Sunshine**

A young mother pays a visit to a doctor friend and his wife but makes no attempt whatsoever to restrain her five-year-old son as he goes into an adjoining room and starts ransacking the place. Finally, an extra loud clatter of bottles prompts the young mother to say, "Oh dear. I hope you don't mind Johnny being in the next room there, doctor." "No, no," says the doctor calmly, "He'll calm down in a minute when he gets to the poisons."

Little Bradley has just gone back to school after the summer holidays when his mother gets a phone call from the headteacher. "I'm just phoning to say that Bradley's behaviour today has been completely unacceptable, and I think we need to discuss it," says the headteacher. The mother is outraged by this. "Unacceptable?" she splutters. "How dare you ring me to tell me my son's behaviour is unacceptable! I have had him here at home for an entire six weeks solid, and I haven't phoned you up to complain about his unacceptable behaviour once!"

Little Kevin goes up to bed but five minutes later he's out of bed again and calling down for his mum to bring him a glass of water. "No," she says, "Just go to sleep." Another five minutes later and Kevin's back at the top of the stairs calling out again for a glass of water. "No," says his mum, "It's really late. Just go sleep now!" Five more minutes pass by and Kevin's calling out again for a glass of water. "Right! That's it!" yells his mum. "You just get to sleep right now before I come up to smack your bottom!" There's a slight pause, then, "Mum," says Kevin, "When you come up to smack my bottom, can you bring a glass of water with you?"

Trying to dress an active little one is a bit like trying to thread a sewing machine while it's running.

"All of us have moments in our lives that test our courage. Taking children into a house with white carpet is one of them."

Erma Bombeck

A mum put her children to bed and then got changed into some old slacks and a droopy blouse so she could go and wash her hair. While she was in the bathroom, she heard the children beginning to mess around and fight and getting noisier and noisier. Eventually she'd had enough so she threw a towel around her head, stormed back into their room, snatched them up and shoved them back in their beds with a stern warning. As she was going out of the room, she heard her three-year-old say in a trembling voice, "Who was that?"

Advice for mum: when you're feeling stressed after a hard day with the kids and you've got a splitting headache, hand them over to Dad then carefully follow the instructions on the Aspirin bottle: "Take two and keep away from children."

My mum was good to me. She stopped me biting my nails – by chopping off my fingers.

We had our home completely child-proofed three years ago but it's no good. They still manage to get in somewhere.

A mother is getting dinner ready one evening while her little boy is playing with his train set in the room next door. She hears him making train noises and then pretending to be the guard on the train giving instructions to the passengers. "Ok you miserable lot – any of you whingeing gits who wants to get off the train you'd better do it now. Hey! It's the last stop so get your fat backsides off my train! Come on! And any of you gormless sods who want to make the return journey, get your backsides in gear right now or we're going without you!" The boy's mother comes in and says "Joseph, that's a terrible way to speak to people. Where on earth did you learn that sort of language? I think you'd better go to your room and come back when you've learned to speak a bit more nicely." So the boy goes to his room and comes out half an hour later. "Well Joseph, are you going to play nicely now?" asks his mother. The boy says yes and starts playing with his train set again while the mother finishes off making dinner and keeps an ear out. "We are now arriving at our destination," says the boy, "Would all passengers please disembark as the train terminates here. Please remember to take your belongings with you and have a safe and pleasant journey. All passengers making the return journey, please wait for passengers to disembark and please accept our apologies for the delay, but if you do wish to make a complaint go and see the bitch in the kitchen."

"I don't think [my six children] had a deprived childhood, exactly, but I think I had a deprived motherhood."

Alice Thomas Ellis

A mum says to her friend, "My kids make me want to jump for joy... off an extremely tall building."

At school in a lesson about religion, the teacher was telling her class of five and six year olds about the Ten Commandments. The teacher explained to them about the commandment about how you should "honour thy father and thy mother." Then she asked if any of the children knew if there was another commandment that told us how we should treat their brothers and sisters. A little boy put his hand up and said, "Thou shalt not kill."

> **"I always sing a song my mother taught me. When it's cold and stormy, and you're feeling a little sick, cuddle up nice and warmy, and play with your little dick. Actually I don't think it was my mother that taught me that. I think it was a boy at school."**
>
> **Hugo Horton, The Vicar of Dibley**

When Jean and her family moved into a new area they were keen to get on with the neighbours, but the people next door just didn't seem to want to know them. Every time Jean saw anyone from next door she was ignored, and even her children were given the cold shoulder. After a few weeks, her son Kieran came running in to see his mum one day. "Mum, guess what? That unfriendly man next door asked what my name was today." "Oh, that's nice" said mum, "I wonder why they've suddenly changed their tune?" "He said he wanted to report me to the police," said Kieran.

Two intrepid explorers meet in the heart of the Brazilian jungle. The first tells the second, "I'm here to commune with nature in the raw, to contemplate the eternal verities and to widen my horizons. And what about you, sir?" "I," sighed the second explorer, "am here because my youngest daughter has just started to have violin lessons."

A man tells his friend, "When I was a little boy I ran away from home and it took my mum and dad six months to find me." "Why so long?" asks his friend. "They didn't bother to look," says the man.

A mum got her young son to go into the Post Office for her, and post a letter in the box. When he came back out of the Post Office he was looking very pleased with himself. "What's the matter with you?" asked his mum. "I just fooled the people at the Post Office," said the little boy. "When no one was looking, I put the letter in the box without buying a stamp for it."

Two mums are talking. The first says, "I finally got my little boy to stop biting his nails." "How did you manage that?" asks the second. "I put his shoes on," says the first.

> **"Like fruit, children are sweetest just before they turn bad."**
>
> **Dena Groquet**

One day, the phone rings in a house and a little boy answers. "Hello," says a voice from the other end of the phone. "Are your mummy and daddy at home?" "Yes," says the little boy. "So can I speak to them?" asks the voice. "No," says the little boy, "They're busy at the moment." "OK," says the voice, "So is anybody else there?" "Yes," says the little boy. "There's the police." "The police?" says the voice. "Well, can I speak to them instead?" "No," says the boy. "They're busy as well." "Oh. OK," says the voice. "So is there anybody else there apart from your mummy and daddy and the police?" "Yes," says the boy. "There's some firemen." "Firemen!" says the voice. "Well, can I speak to them?" "No," says the boy, "They're busy too." "OK," says the voice, "So let me get this straight. Your parents, the police, and the firemen are all there at your house at the moment, but they're all too busy to come to the phone? What are they doing?" "Looking for me," whispers the little boy.

When little Harry sees his Auntie Alison after Christmas he thanks her for the drum kit she bought him. "It's fantastic," he enthused, "It's the best present I've ever had." "So," said his aunt, "I bet you have lots of fun playing on it." "Oh I've only ever played on it once," says Harry, "But my mum gives me a pound a day not to play it, and she doubles the rate for the evenings."

There was a little boy who didn't speak a word for years. His parents were really worried and called on all manner of doctors, psychiatrists and speech therapists to help but without success. Then one day when he was eight years old he finally spoke his first ever words when he told his mum, "Mummy, my chips are cold." His mum was completely amazed. "Good heavens!" she said. "We didn't know you could talk. Why haven't you said anything until now?" "Because," said the little boy, "up until now everything's been OK."

Little Jimmy comes home one day with a brand-new football. "Where did you get that football?" asks his mum. "I found it in the street," says Jimmy proudly bouncing the ball up and down. "Someone must have lost it." "Are you sure it was lost?" asks his mum suspiciously. "Yeah, of course I am," says Jimmy. "I saw three boys looking for it."

At one point during a football game, the coach says to one of his young players, "Do you understand what cooperation is? Do you understand what a team is?" The little boy nods in the affirmative. "Do you understand," says the coach, "that what matters is whether we win together as a team?" Again the little boy nods yes. "So," the coach continues, "if a goal is disallowed or a penalty is given against you, you don't argue or swear or suddenly attack the referee or linesman. Do you understand that now?" Again the little boy nods. "Excellent," says the coach. "Now please could you go over there and explain all that to your mother."

> **"Never underestimate a child's ability to get into more trouble."**
>
> **Martin Mull**

Much advice has been passed down from generation to generation, but don't worry, it's never been used.

Why is it parents always take their children to supermarkets to smack them?

A woman on the phone to her friend had two extremely lively and noisy young daughters. Their conversation was constantly being interrupted by the noise of the kids shouting, chasing after one another and screaming. In the end the mother said, "Hang on. This is no good. Just wait a moment." Her friend heard the phone put down and then after a few moments all the screaming and shouting stopped completely. "Hi, I'm back," said the mum picking the phone up again. "Wow! I'm really impressed!" says the friend. "You must have incredible control over your girls. I can't hear them at all now." "I know," says the mother. "I'm inside the wardrobe."

Three young sons of a farmer manage to open their father's locked cupboard and start playing with his rifle and ammunition. Each one of them dares the other to swallow a bullet, and then their mother catches them and asks them what they've done. Sheepishly they explain and the mother tells them that although what they've done is very bad, the bullets will eventually go through their systems and be harmlessly passed when they go to the toilet. A couple of days later the first boy goes to his mother and says "You were right Mum, when I went to the toilet this morning it was a bit painful, but that bullet came out at last." "Good," says the mother, "I hope it teaches you a lesson." Then the second boy comes and explains that he too has passed a bullet. A while later the third son comes to his mother. "Don't tell me," she says, "You've passed a bullet as well." "No mum," says the boy, "It's worse than that. I just farted and shot dad in the leg."

"My mother had a great deal of trouble with me, but I think she enjoyed it."

Mark Twain

A little girl received a brand new watch and a bottle of perfume for her Christmas presents. She was so proud of these she went round all her family sticking the watch in their ear and insisting that they smell her perfume. Mum, Dad and her brothers and sisters got so fed up with this that Mum told her, "If you mention that watch or that perfume once more when all the rest of the family turn up for dinner, I'm going to send you to your room for the rest of the day." All the relatives then turned up and Christmas dinner went well. The little girl didn't says anything until just as the pudding was being served she piped up and said loudly in front of all the relatives, "By the way, if you hear anything or smell anything... it's me!"

"The hardest job facing kids today is learning good manners without seeing any."

Fred Astaire

Mum notices five-year-old Damien taking his little sister's sweets. "Damien, I hope you're not taking your little sister's sweets are you?" "No," says Damien, "I'm teaching her how to share."

Did you hear about the mother sheep who caught her little lamb doing something naughty and told him, "Do you know what, if your father could see you doing that he'd turn in his gravy."

A woman phoned up her convalescing friend to see how she was. The phone was answered by her seven-year-old son, who was speaking in a very quiet voice. "Hello, Philip, how's your mum?" asked the friend. "She's OK I think," whispered Philip. "She's asleep at the moment." "OK," says the friend, "I must say you're being a very good boy speaking quietly so you don't wake her up." "That's right," whispered Philip. "So what are you doing, reading a book or drawing or something?" "No," said Philip, "I'm just practising on my electric guitar."

A swimming pool lifeguard comes up to a young mother and says, "Excuse me. If your child urinates in the pool again, I will have to ask the pair of you to leave." "I'm sorry," says the mother, "but he's only a little boy and small children sometimes can't help themselves from weeing in the pool." "I know," says the lifeguard, "but your son keeps doing it from the top diving board."

Mum was upstairs in the bathroom when the phone rang and little Freddie answered it. As he'd been taught to, he asked who was calling so that his mum could call them back. The woman said her name was Vicky and decided she'd better spell it for him. "That's V for violin," she said, "I for ice-cream, C for cat, K for kite, and Y for yacht." When Freddie's mum came down his mum asked who had phoned. "It was a lady with a funny name." said Freddie. "Oh really?" said his mum. "Can you remember what it was?" "Oh yes," said Freddie. "It was Violinicecreamcatkiteyacht."

"I love all my children, but some of them I don't like."

Lillian Carter

Two little boys are talking. One says to the other, "If you broke your arm in two places, what would you do?" The other replies, "I wouldn't go back to those two places."

An irate mother bursts into a baker's shop and says, "I sent my son in here for two pounds of cookies this morning, but when he got home and I weighed them there was only one pound. I suggest that you check your scales." The baker looks at her calmly for a moment or two and then replies, "Madam, I suggest you weigh your son."

Little Ben runs to his mother. "Mum, can I get my name changed in a hurry please?" he asks. "But why would you want to do that, dear?" asks his mum. "Cause Dad says he's going to spank me as sure as my name's Benjamin!"

A man is walking round the supermarket when he sees a young mother with her three-year-old daughter doing their shopping. As they pass the bakery, the child asks for some cakes but her mother tells "No." The little girl immediately begins to whine and whinge but the mother stays calm and says quietly, "Now Ellen, don't start getting upset. We've not got much more to get. It won't be long. Then you can go home." The man passes the mother in the confectionary aisle where, of course, the little girl is kicking up a huge fuss for some chocolate. Again the mother calmly tells her no but when the child starts screaming and crying she stays completely calm and says, "Now, now, Ellen. No need to cry. Just a couple more things to get then we can go home." The man ends up just behind the pair at the check-out, where the little girl is now raising the roof screaming for some sweeties but the mother still stays completely calm and says, "Ellen, calm down now. We'll be out of here in a couple of minutes then you can go home and have a lovely little nap until you feel better." As they follow each other out into the car park the man remarks to the mother, "I have to say I really admire how you kept so calm going round the supermarket just now and how patiently you spoke to your little daughter Ellen. And the mother says, "What do you mean 'my little daughter Ellen'? My daughter's name is Jessica. I'm Ellen."

Until I was 13, I thought my name was "Shuttup".

A salesman knocks at a house. The door opens up and there, standing in the hall, is a ten-year-old boy smoking a cigar, with a glass of brandy in his hand and a copy of *Fiesta Readers Wives* under his arm. "Hi, sonny," says the salesman. "Is your mummy at home?" And the little boy taps some ash off his cigar and says, "What the hell do you think?"

My mother never saw the irony in calling me a son-of-a-bitch.

> **"There never was a child so lovely but his mother was glad to get him asleep."**
>
> **Ralph Waldo Emerson**

A salesman sees a young boy sitting on the step and says, "Hello there, little feller. So is your mummy at home?" "Yes she is," says the little boy. So the salesman steps past him and spends the next five minutes ringing on the bell and knocking on the door over and over again, but never getting any answer. Finally in frustration, he turns back to the boy and says, "What's going on? I thought you said your mummy was at home." "She is," says the boy. "We live across the street."

A little boy shouts to his mother, “Mummy! Mummy! Do you know the beautiful vase in the dining room that’s been handed down from generation to generation?” “Yes,” says his mummy. “What about it?” The little boy replies, “Well the last generation has just dropped it.”

One day Jeremy was playing football in the house, which was strictly against the rules, when he accidentally broke a vase in the living room. “Oh, no, my mum’s going to kill me!” he thought desperately. So he frantically tried to fix the vase, any way he could. But tape, glue, even Superglue wouldn’t hold all the shards together. So he finally left the pieces in a pile on the table and went and tried to hide in his room. Soon his mum came home and he heard her calling him: “Jeremy! Jeremy! Do you know who broke my vase? It’s in here all in pieces!” Jeremy tried to drum up his courage, but at the last minute, he found himself answering, “No, mummy, I don’t know,” he cringed waiting for her answer. “That’s funny,” she said, appearing at his door. “I wanted to thank whoever it was. I’ve hated that thing for years.”

As a crowded airliner is about to take off, the peace is shattered by a five-year-old boy who picks that moment to throw a wild temper tantrum. No matter what his frustrated, embarrassed mother does to try to calm him down, the boy continues to scream furiously and kick the seats around him. Suddenly, from the rear of the plane, an elderly man in the uniform of an Air Force General is seen slowly walking forward up the aisle. Stopping the flustered mother with an upraised hand, the white-haired, courtly, soft-spoken General leans down and, motioning toward his chest, whispers something into the boy’s ear. Instantly, the boy calms down, gently takes his mother’s hand, and quietly fastens his seat belt. All the other passengers burst into spontaneous applause. As the General slowly makes his way back to his seat, one of the cabin attendants touches his sleeve. “Excuse me, General,” she asks quietly, “but could I ask you what magic words you used on that little boy?” The old man smiles serenely and gently confides, “I showed him my pilot’s wings, service stars, and battle ribbons, and explained that they entitle me to throw one passenger out the plane door on any flight I choose.”

Of course you know even God had trouble with his kids. Remember Adam and Eve in the Garden of Eden? One of the first things God had to say to his children was "Don't!" just like you do with yours. "Don't what?" asked Adam, all innocent (just like yours). "Don't eat the forbidden fruit," said God. "Oh, I didn't know it was forbidden," said Adam, thinking that that made it twice as attractive (just like yours). He called out to Eve: "Hey, Eve, over here – forbidden fruit." "Wow!" said Eve, grabbing an apple. "Don't eat it!" commanded God. "Well he's had some!" protested Eve. "It is forbidden to eat the fruit." said God. "He started it." said Eve. (recognise any of this Mum?) "I didn't!" snapped Adam. "Oh yes you did!" replied Eve. "Didn't!" "Did!" "Didn't!" "Did!" "Didn't, didn't, didn't!" shouted Adam. Just like you, Mum, God wondered then whether he should just bang their heads together. But then he thought of a far better punishment: he let them have children of their own.

You Know You're A Mum When...

- You think that eating a meal in one sitting (without ever getting up) is something people only ever do in the movies.
- You prefer to browse the toy section rather than the adult clothing department of any given superstore.
- Every window in the house that is below three feet high has permanent grease marks.
- Even your new car smells like sour milk.
- Every pair of trousers you own has a stain on the thighs from holding persons with very dirty sandbox feet.
- You think planning a date with your partner two weeks in advance is being spontaneous.

- You think staying up past 10pm is way too late.
- You have replaced your "completion complex" with a satisfied grin every time you manage to empty your dish washer within five attempts.
- You dream of wiping, wiping, wiping.
- You never sniff the wash anymore to determine its level of dirtiness – if it found its way to the laundry room, you don't ask questions!
- You can't remember the PIN to your on-line checking account, but you can recite all the names of the seven dwarfs from Snow White.
- You start to wonder why friends and family don't visit as much any more and never, ever spend the night (they value their sleep, too!).
- You actually want to go to the zoo.

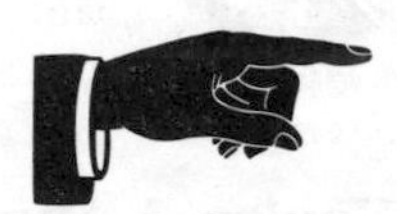

Techniques For Disciplining Children

Time out

This means either making misbehaving children leave the room for a little while until they calm down or, if that fails, bribing them using a Time Out chocolate bar.

Putting the child on the naughty step

The problem with this technique is that children may decide not to stay on the naughty step and will return to the living room or kitchen from which you have just removed them. This will thereby turn the living room or kitchen into the naughty living room or naughty kitchen.

To ensure children don't leave the naughty step of their own accord, try making the naughty step somewhere in the region of 20 or 30 naughty feet high.

Children should then stay on the naughty step until you come to allow them back in to the room. Unless, of course, there is a sudden strong naughty breeze.

Withholding pocket money

Of course as pocket money is usually a child's sole source of income they may turn this back on you on your birthday when they say they couldn't buy you a present because they didn't have any money.

Grounding them

In other words making them stay at home instead of going out with their friends. As the few precious hours when they are out with their friends is the only time you get a bit of peace and quiet you're actually punishing yourself by using this method.

Pretending to be mortified at their bad behaviour

The "how could you do this to me?", "what kind of child have I brought into the world?" tack will probably be seen as a badge of honour amongst their friends and siblings and will start a competitive spiral of bad behaviour amongst the lot of them.

Use natural consequences

Using natural consequences does not mean that if your child misbehaves you put them outside in the rain for the afternoon.

Instead, if your child, for example, throws a toy out of the window that means they won't have the toy to play with any more. This does not mean that if your child throws a toy out of the window you then throw the child out of the window after it.

Put a chart up on the wall and give them a sticker for good behaviour

It's amazing how easy it is to raise kids' esteem and bribe them into behaving well just by offering them a colourful sticker by way of reward. This use of essentially worthless bits of paper as a means to make children fall into line and fit in with society around them is then analogous to the use of money in the adult world.

Stare into their eyes

Stop your child's errant behaviour by saying "no" while staring firmly into their eyes. Do this for long enough and you may find you have hypnotized them and they will remain perfectly behaved for the next few years' of their childhood until, on their 18th birthday, you snap your fingers and tell them they're "back in the room".

Of course if you stare into their eyes for long enough you may find that they hypnotize you by mistake. You will then spend the next portion of your life as the glassy eyed, mesmerized slave who must perform the every bidding of a small child.

You Might Be A Mum Who Sets A Bad Example If...

- You positively encourage your children to have cosmetic breast enlargement so they'll look like Jordan – even the boys.
- You tell the kids the onion in cheese and onion flavour crisps counts as one of their five vegetable portions a day.
- You pretend that the reason you live on benefits and refuse to get a job is so that you can spend more time with them.
- You refuse to wear a seatbelt in the car so that's it's easier to turn round and give them a clip round the ear while you're driving.
- You tell them you're trying to protect them by carrying on smoking so there won't be any cigarettes left by the time they're old enough to be able to buy them for themselves.
- You swear in front of them so they won't keep asking what those words mean when you let them watch 18 certificate films.

- On their birth certificate where it says name of father you have filled in multiple choice-style options.
- Before they are even born you have staked the entire child benefit payments you will receive over the next 18 years on a massive accumulator bet.

Advice From Kids On Romantic Issues

"When they're rich."

Girl aged seven (when asked when it's acceptable to kiss someone)

"It gives me a headache to think about that stuff. I'm just a kid. I don't need that kind of trouble."

Boy aged seven (when asked about kissing)

"When a person gets kissed for the first time, they fall down, and they don't get up for at least an hour."

Girl aged eight (on kissing)

"You should never kiss a girl unless you have enough bucks to buy her a big ring and her own video recorder, 'cause she'll want to have videos of the wedding."

Boy aged ten (on kissing)

"Never kiss in front of other people. It's a big embarrassing thing if anybody sees you. But if nobody sees you, I might be willing to try it with a handsome boy, but just for a few hours."

Girl aged nine (on kissing)

"You learn right on the spot when the gooshy feelings get the best of you."

Boy aged seven (on learning how to kiss)

The Most Annoying Things That Mums Do

Getting out embarrassing photos of you when your boyfriend/girlfriend visits on a first date

Looking at pictures of yourself aged two either stark naked and rolling in fat or dressed in something ludicrous is not the preferred image you wish the love of your life to take away with them when they are deciding whether to see you for a second time.

Straightening your clothes and combing your hair when dropping you at school

They have all morning to do this in the privacy of your home, but no, they wait until you're in front of all your friends and then decide to embarrass you. As if that weren't enough they then demand a big sloppy kiss before they go.

Serving up leftovers

Mums love doing this. Each night the family turns up for a freshly cooked dinner (not that any of them are prepared to help freshly cook it) and what do they get? An unrequested encore of the previous night's meal. A plateful of something that looks familiar but which is now slightly darker and moves around less easily than it used to – a bit like an elderly relative who has just returned from many years spent in foreign climes.

Finding daughter's boyfriends attractive

Mums with teenage daughters will often comment on how attractive they find any boys who are brought home. The subtext is clear – given half a chance mum will ditch dad to run off with someone 25 years her junior even if they're covered in acne from head to foot.

Comparing your kids to other children

Unfortunately this only works one way. They say things like "Why can't you be top of the class like Tom", or "Why can't you stay out of trouble like Dick", or "Why don't you dress smartly like Harry?" They never say, "Why haven't you got a criminal record like Dwayne?"

Picking bits off the kids

Mums of all ages are constantly picking bits off their children's shoulders, back, heads, you name it. Somehow the mums' superhuman vision has picked up tiny particles of dirt and dust that no other living creature armed with anything less than an electron microscope would be able to see, even in a good light.

Mum will nevertheless spot these tiny specks in an instant. They will then set about the apparently unending work of picking them off one by one despite the fact that this will give observers the impression that their offspring are overrun by some form of microscopic parasite.

Cleaning the kids' faces with a spitty hanky

What kind of a lesson in hygiene is this, mum?

You spot a microscopic speck of dirt on the brow of one of your little loved ones. Then in order to clean it off you dip into your bag or pocket and do you produce a clean, fresh, moist, lemon scented cleaning square?

No you don't!

Instead you yank out your grey grimy old hanky (possibly already caked in goodness knows what) which you then proceed to turn into something resembling a cleaning square by moistening with your own naturally produced sputum.

Yes, just to make sure this already stained and slimy piece of cloth is really going to remove that atom of mud from your child's cheek, you gob into it a couple of times and then slap the whole extraordinary creation slap bang onto your offspring's nose and revolve it a few times all over their horrified little face.

Kids' Behaviour Round the House

The perfect mother	The slightly imperfect mother	The mother who should not be allowed near children
They help mum with the cleaning regularly	They help mum with the cleaning if they're bribed	They do all the cleaning
They're on their best behaviour all the time	They're on their best behaviour when visitors come	They behave a bit better when the social worker comes to assess their benefits
They look after their pets	They look after their pets when reminded	They make friends with the rats as they're not actually allowed proper pets

Kids' Behaviour Round The Neighbourhood

The perfect mother	The slightly imperfect mother	The mother who should not be allowed near children
The neighbours love them	The neighbours put up with them	The neighbours have invested in window grills and fire-resistant front doors
Shopkeepers remark on their good manners	Shopkeepers put up with them	Shopkeepers have had to increase their insurance cover just because of them
The police have no idea who they are	The police have had a word with them once or twice	The police will now only speak to them if they have back-up

Attention Children!

The Bathroom Door is Closed.

Please do not stand here and talk, whine, or ask questions. Wait until I get out.

Yes, it is locked. I want it that way. It is not broken, I am not trapped. I know I have left it unlocked, and even open at times, since you were born, because I was afraid some horrible tragedy might occur while I was in here, but it's been ten years and I want some PRIVACY.

Do not ask me how long I will be. I will come out when I am done.

Do not bring the phone to the bathroom door.

Do not go running back to the phone yelling, "She's in the BATHROOM!"

Do not begin to fight as soon as I go in.

Do not stick your little fingers under the door and wiggle them. This was funny when you were two, but not now.

Do not slide pennies, Lego bricks, or notes under the door. Even when you were two this got a little tiresome.

If you have followed me down the hall talking, and are still talking as you face this closed door, please turn around, walk away, and wait for me in another room. I will be glad to listen to you when I am done.

OK, yes, I still love you.

(signed)
Mummy

Other Peoples' Kids

Other people's kids are a funny lot – they do better than your kids in exams, they have better manners, and they look smarter and cleaner than your rabble, but other people's kids are also the scum of the earth, teaching your kids swearwords, getting them into trouble with the police, leading them astray and piling on the peer group pressure with their £150 trainers, their state-of-the-art computer games consoles, their designer clothes and their smug immunity from head lice. In short, other people's kids are a pain in the neck. So perhaps you should count yourself lucky your lot are only slightly imperfect.

Mumly wisdom: One of the main reasons to hold a children's party is to remind yourself that there are children out there who are even worse than your own – and you can send them home at the end of it.

One morning a woman has to go round to her neighbour's house to look after the neighbour's small son. She arrives in time to make breakfast and cooks up bacon, eggs and toast which she presents to the little boy. The little boy looks at the bacon, eggs and toast, sniffs and says, "That's not what mummy makes me for my breakfast. Mummy always makes me porridge." "OK," says the good neighbour. "No problem. I'll go and make you some porridge then." So she goes back out into the kitchen, cooks up a lovely big bowl of steaming hot porridge, brings it back to the little boy and places it in front of him. "Yuk!" says the little boy looking like he's about to throw up. "What do you mean 'Yuk'?" asks the neighbour. "I thought you said your mother always makes you porridge in the morning!" "She does," says the little boy. "But I never eat it."

A young man agrees to babysit one night so a single mother can have an evening out. At bedtime he sends all the youngsters upstairs to bed and settles down to watch football on TV. One child keeps annoying him by creeping down the stairs over and over again. Each time the young man chases the child back upstairs and tells him to stay there. Finally at nine o'clock there's a knock on the door and there on the step is the next-door neighbour. "Have you got my son here?" she demands. "What are you talking about?" says the man. "Of course I haven't." But then he hears a little voice from the top of the stairs calling, "I'm here, mummy! But the bad man won't let me come home!"

A six-year-old boy comes back from playing at his friend Charlie's house and tells his mother there's some good news and bad news. "Oh," says his mum. "What's the bad news?" "I threw a football in Charlie's front room," says the little boy, "and it knocked over a lamp and broke it." "And the good news?" asks his mother, sighing. "You don't have to worry about buying his mum another one," says the little boy, "because she said it was irreplaceable."

A little boy knocks on the front door of his friend's house. His friend's mum answers and he asks, "Can Albert come out to play?" "I'm sorry," says Albert's mum. "It's too cold today." "OK," says the little boy. "Can his football come out to play?"

How Other Peoples' Kids Can Be A Pain In The Neck

Your kids constantly use them as yardsticks by which to measure their own deprived childhoods – he's got a new PlayStation, she's got a Bluetooth mobile, they're going to Disneyland for their holidays, etc., etc.

There's always at least one who's doing better than yours in exams, getting better marks, or generally being a sickening goody-goody.

They report back to their mums on how you've got dust on the tops of your cupboards, a washing basket piled high with dirty clothes, and you dish up left-overs for tea.

They know swear words your children don't and they insist on teaching them.

Have you noticed how it's always someone else's kids who spreads flu bugs, tummy bugs and head lice? If it wasn't for other people's kids they'd all be healthy!

Thank God your kids aren't other people's kids!

Why Other Peoples' Kids Are Easier To Entertain Than Your Own Kids

They are forced to be polite when they come to your house.

They will gratefully eat whatever they are given.

When they misbehave you know it's not your fault.

Any rude words they might utter certainly weren't learnt from you.

If they behave well you can use them as an example for your kids.

If they behave badly you can feel smug that yours aren't as bad as that.

They say thank you for their meal.

They ask permission before they do anything.

If they get food down their clothes you won't have to wash it out.

You can send them home at the end of their stay.

How Other People's Kids Can Be Plain Wonderful

They do their homework.

They win awards.

They are a credit to their families and their school.

They are respectful to you when they visit.

You never have to deal with them late at night or first thing in the morning.

Why can't your kids be like other people's kids?

Things Other Peoples' Kids Will Do To Drive You Crazy While You're Looking After Them

They will give you a detailed lecture on how every aspect of what you are doing would be done completely differently and so much better by their mummy.

The moment they get inside your house they will demand to go home. However much you may wish to comply with this request, you are stuck with them and then have to spend the next two hours trying to bribe them with goodies, entertain them and retain the patience of the most saintly saint imaginable.

They will give you intimate details of their home life and the behaviour of their parents that leave you wondering whether to take them home afterwards or just drop them straight round with social services.

They will inform you of the many food allergies they suffer from, approximately 30 seconds after you've fed them a potentially lethal snack.

Like junior bailiffs they will march round the house opening cupboards, picking up and inspecting anything which looks a) extremely valuable and b) extremely breakable. You will therefore be compelled to follow them around twitching nervously and with a feeling of dread in the pit of your stomach.

They will have an argument with, or physically assault your child in the full knowledge that you, as the arbiter in all domestic disputes, will have to give them the benefit of the doubt in order to appear impartial.

They will follow you around providing you with the wit and wisdom of their mother in a series of quotations prefaced by the word "My mummy says..." Clearly it will not be long before the world accepts their mummy as some kind of female equivalent of Confucius, Buddha, and Jesus – but slightly more irritating.

They will give your house plants a vigorous pruning, leaving you with a few bare stalks by the time they go home.

They will quickly and dramatically re-design the layout of your living room for you as though they're some kind of miniature Laurence Llewellyn-Bowen.

They will refuse to eat anything you put in front of them and you will end up giving them the sort of junk which you know they will devour, thereby getting yourself branded as a failed mother in the playground next day.

Just when you think you're about to get rid of them, before you finally give up and strangle them, they bound up to you with your child and announce they've just arranged a sleepover.

You Might Be An Over Protective Mum If...

- You're persist in using baby monitors to check on your children even after they've grown up and left home.
- You enquire at your local vets if it's possible to get your kids micro-chipped like your pets.
- The kitchen knives are in a glass "break in emergency" case.
- If you have to go out for the evening you give the babysitter a 50 page instruction booklet plus a ten minute Powerpoint presentation covering the main points.
- You're on first name terms with the A&E staff at the local hospital.
- If your child wants to go outside on a sunny day you use a paint roller to apply their sun block.
- You make any friends they're going out to play with fill in a health and safety compliance form first.
- You won't let them have roller skates until their 18th birthday.
- You make them put on scarf, gloves and bobble hat before they're allowed to open the fridge.
- You make them wear a crash helmet when you put them in the baby seat on a supermarket trolley.
- You surreptitiously do full background security checks on their friends, friends' parents, teachers, school governors, babysitters and, last but not least, their father.

Films Possibly About Mums

The Mummy

Mother's Day

Mummy's Hand

Return of the Mummy (strange how they're all horror films so far isn't it?)

Mommie Dearest

Mother (Mat) – shouldn't that be 'doormat'?

Mother Wore Tights

Mother, Jugs and Speed

Mother Kuster's Trip to Heaven

Mr Mom (hey, we like the sound of that don't we?)

Mrs Miniver

Mrs Soffel

The Good, The Bad and the Ugly: Answers Mums Give to Kids' Questions

Mummy, why is that person begging for money?

Good response – Because he has not been as fortunate in life as we have.

Bad response – Because he's a drug addict and/or alcoholic and/or just plain lazy.

Ugly response – Because he's a loser. And just to prove it, I'll distract him while you snatch the money from his cap.

Mummy, why is that person so fat?

Good response – Because they have a glandular problem.
Bad response – Because they eat too many cakes.
Ugly response – Because they have eaten several small children.

Mummy, why is that person dribbling and talking to themselves?

Good response – Because they have a mental problem and find the world very difficult to cope with.
Bad response – Because they're a loony.
Ugly response – Because they've had children of their own and this is the result.

Mummy, why is that man lying in the gutter?

Good response – He's probably a bit tired, dear.
Bad response – He's drunk too much and fallen over.
Ugly response – He died because he wouldn't eat his broccoli.

Mummy, where did I come from?

Good response – You came from Mummy's tummy.
Bad response – You were delivered by the stork.
Ugly response – I found you on the doorstep and if you keep on asking stupid questions I'm going to put you back there.

Mummy, are fizzy drinks bad for you?

Good response – Yes, they're full of sugar and rot your teeth.
Bad response – Only if you have too many.
Ugly response – No, and mine's a gin and tonic.

Mummy, why is that person threatening us and asking for money?

Good response – Because they are a victim of an oppressive society.
Bad response – They're evil and they want your pocket money.
Ugly response – No use threatening me, matey! The kids are the ones with all the cash!

Mummy, is driving our car bad for the environment?

Good response – Well, we should try and keep our journeys to a minimum.
Bad response – Very bad, and from now on we'll try to cycle everywhere.
Ugly response – Stuff the environment, I'm not travelling on a bus for anyone.

Mums and Food

You spend the first half of their childhood trying to encourage your children to eat things, and the second half trying to get them to stop. There seems to be no middle ground. They're either fussy faddy food refuseniks or ravenous beasts engaged in a 24-hour scoff-a-thon with the fridge door permanently open like a circus lion's mouth with someone's head in it. And in between times they may decide to go vegetarian, cut out carbohydrates, shun sugar or only want to eat fair trade products, which would be fine-ish if there was only one of them, but if you've got two or three, or more, each with his or her own food fetishes, then it makes the feeding of the 5,000 look like a bit of a doddle.

> **"There are times when parenthood seems nothing but feeding the mouth that bites you."**
>
> **Peter de Vries**

Sign seen in a baker's window: "Cakes like your mum used to make – £2. Cakes like she thinks she used to make - £10."

Get your children to eat greens by dyeing the broccoli red.

If you've got a child who won't eat spinach, but will eat carrots, and you've got a child who will eat carrots but refuses to eat spinach, then simply swap their plates halfway through the meal.

"I was born because my mother needed a fourth for meals."

Beatrice Lillie

A little boy has to say grace before dinner is served. He thanks God for all his friends, thanks God for his mummy, daddy, brother, sister, grandma and grandpa, his aunts, his uncles and his whole extended family. Then he moves on to thank God for the wonderful food. He thanks God for the meat, he thanks God for the potatoes, he thanks God for the gravy and he thanks God for the pudding that's coming afterwards. "That's very good, son," says his mummy. "But you forgot to thank God for the broccoli didn't you?" "I know," says the little boy. "But if I thank him for the broccoli, won't he know I'm lying?"

Q: What's the difference between bogies and broccoli?
A: Kids will eat bogies.

A little boy tells his friend, "My mum's cooking isn't so much cordon bleu as cordon noir."

Interviewer: "Tell me Prime Minister, do you ever get to have a meal with your family?"
Prime Minister: "Yes, as long as my mother isn't cooking!"

Mum is a terrible cook. She once tried making a cottage pie and it was condemned.

"This would be a better world for children if parents had to eat the spinach."

Groucho Marx

Never let dad near the cooker! On Mother's Day he tried cooking me a casserole. After I'd managed to force it down he asked me what I wanted for pudding. I said, "The antidote."

Two mums are talking. The first says, "My husband Derek never criticises my cooking." "You're lucky," says the second. "Not really," says the first, "he just looks at his plate and says something like, 'What's the problem? Wasn't the cat hungry?'"

> **"The most remarkable thing about my mother is that for thirty years she served the family nothing but leftovers. The original meal has never been found."**
>
> **Calvin Trillin**

A little boy comes down to breakfast and sees his sister eating a bowl of mum's best porridge. "Oh no," says the little boy, "You're not going to eat that are you?" Then he looks at it again and says, "Or maybe you did already?"

Mum and Dad go to gran's for dinner and the food, as usual, is terrible. Dad whispers to Mum, "You know, I hate to say this again but your mum is a really terrible cook – this pie is like a cow pat." "No, it's not," says Mum, "I want you to take that back at once." Dad thinks for a moment and says "You know love, you're right. It isn't really like a cow pat. A cow pat's usually at least a little bit warm."

> **"Most turkeys taste better the day after; my mother's tasted better the day before."**
>
> **Rita Rudner**

What's the difference between an Italian mother and a Jewish mother? The Italian mother says, "If you don't eat your dinner I'll kill you." The Jewish mother says, "If you don't eat your dinner I'll kill myself."

Dad to kids: "Mum woke me up the other night and told me there was a burglar in the kitchen eating some of her left-over curry. I didn't know who to call first, the police or a doctor."

> **"My mother is such a lousy cook that Thanksgiving at her house is a time of sorrow."**
>
> **Rita Rudner**

A mum tells a friend, "Some husbands can cook, but don't. My husband is the exact opposite."

They say that nine out of ten home accidents happen in the kitchen. Unfortunately we usually end up eating most of them.
A mum asks her son, "Would you like a frozen pizza for dinner tonight?" And the little boy replies, "No. I'd prefer it warmed it up if it's all the same to you, mother."

Little Tommy's class go on a trip from school to visit the local fire station. A fireman gives them a talk about how they can stay safe in their own homes during which he holds up a smoke detector and asks them, "OK. Hands up, who knows what this is for?" Little Tommy's hand shoots up and he says, "It's the thing that tells Mummy when our toast is ready!"

> **"Why do mums buy crap pop? Why?... Never Coca Cola, or Pepsi. It's Friendly Cola, Koala Cola, or Steamway Cola. Eight litres for 40p. Crap pop. Shit pop. Pop you don't want. 'Get it drunk!' 'I'm not drinkin' it!' 'Get it drunk!' 'I'm not drinkin' it, Mum. I wouldn't wash me drains out with this! It's crap!' 'There's children starvin' in Ethiopia!' 'Send it to 'em. They'll send it back. They won't drink it. It's crap pop!'"**
>
> **Peter Kay**

The three bears go into their kitchen. "What's going on here?" says the daddy bear. "I've got no porridge. Who's been eating my porridge?" The baby bear peers into his bowl and says, "Look at this! I've got no porridge either! Who's been eating my porridge?" And the mummy bear shouts, "I know you haven't got any porridge. I haven't got round to making it yet! Honestly! Do we have to go through this every single morning?"

Q: Why does mum give dad a lunch box with a transparent lid?
A: So when he's on the bus he can tell if he's going to work or coming home.

A mother is making pancakes and her two sons, Nicholas and Ryan are waiting eagerly for them to cook. The two boys begin to argue about who's going to get the first pancake. Their mother sees the opportunity for a religious lesson. "You know what," she says. "If Jesus was here, he would say, "Let my brother have the first pancake, I can wait." "What a good idea," says Nicholas and turns to his little brother, "Ryan, you be Jesus!"

"My mother's menu consisted of two choices: take it or leave it."

Buddy Hackett

A busy mum's sister helped her have a much needed break. The mum went away for a few days' holiday while the sister stayed behind and looked after her three children. The first night she was there she made them one of their favourite dinners. Then the next night she made them another meal they really liked and so on and on all the time she was there, she cooked them all their favourite food. When the mum returned from her break, she was astonished her sister had been so successful in guessing the kids' tastes. "How did you do it?" she asked. "Simple," said her sister. "I looked through the cook books in your kitchen and just made them all the things on the pages that were ripped, smudged and covered in bits of food."

> **"My cooking is so bad my kids thought Thanksgiving was to commemorate Pearl Harbour."**
>
> **Phyllis Diller**

A child will always eat exactly what she has loved for the past year... unless it is the only food in the fridge.
A mum invites some people to dinner. At the table, she turns to their six-year-old daughter and says, "Do you want to say a prayer before we eat?" "I don't know what to say, Mummy," says the little girl. "Just say what you hear Mummy say," says the mummy. "OK," says the little girl and bows her head and goes on. "Oh Lord, what the hell was I thinking when I invited all these stupid people round for dinner?"

> **"I often put boiling water in the freezer. Then whenever I need boiling water, I simply defrost it."**
>
> **Gracie Allen**

Dad comes home from work famished to find just a piece of apple crumble for his dinner. "Hey, is this it?" he asks Mum, "I thought you said we were having a big three course roast dinner with all the trimmings!" "Well, we were," said Mum, "But then my mum phoned, and you know how she goes on and before I knew it the dinner was burnt, smoke everywhere and I had to use the soup to put out the meat and veg."

> **"A mother is a person who, seeing there are only four pieces of pie for five people, promptly announces she never did care for pie."**
>
> **Tenneva Jordan**

> **"There is just one thing more exasperating than a wife who can cook and won't, and that's a wife who can't cook and will."**
>
> **Robert Frost**

"Mummy, mummy. Why can't we have a waste disposal unit?"
"Shut up and keep chewing."

Cooking Rule... If at first you don't succeed, order pizza.

Q: Why don't Jewish mothers drink?
A: Alcohol interferes with their suffering.

A woman was nervous one night because she and her husband had decided to take their young sons to an expensive restaurant for the first time, and they were worried in case they showed them up in some way. When they placed their order the husband requested a bottle of wine with the meal and when the waiter brought it to the table, the children became quiet as he began the uncorking ritual. The waiter poured a small amount for the wife to taste and handed it over to her, at which point the couple's six-year-old piped up, "Mum usually drinks a whole lot more than that!"

> **"Dessert is probably the most important stage of the meal, since it will be the last thing your guests remember before they pass out all over the table."**
>
> **The Anarchist Cookbook**

A mum was having dinner when the phone rang. The mum was so busy trying to get some tomato ketchup to come out of the bottle, she had to ask her four-year-old daughter to get the phone for her. The vicar was on the line. So Mum was really pleased to hear her daughter telling him, "Mummy can't come to the phone to talk to you right now. She's just hitting the bottle."

A boy goes to the shops and sees a Thermos flask for the first time. He asks the man what it does. "It keeps hot things hot and cold things cold," he replies. So the boy buys one with his pocket money and takes it to school the next day. "Look," he says to one of his friends. "It's amazing, it's called a Thermos flask and it keeps hot things hot and cold things cold," "What have you got in it?" says his friend. "A cup of hot chocolate and an ice lolly."

"My mum had a system for feeding us: the 'Scoop-Chop System', you're probably familiar with it. Up until the age of five, we were allocated one scoop of mash and one chop. From the ages of five to eight, we were allocated two scoops of mash, and one chop, or the fish-finger equivalent. From the age of eight onwards, we were allocated two scoops of mash, two chops. That was the top level. You could be 16, you could be 60 - two scoops, two chops. Well, you can imagine, you get to about 30 or 31, and you want a little more mash. So one night, we snuck into her kitchen, and we substituted her mash scoop for one ever-so-slightly larger. That night she's dolling out mash, unbeknownst to her, from a slightly larger scoop. We're getting a tiny bit of extra mash! The next night, we substituted that scoop for one ever-so-slightly larger... Three years later she's dolling out mash from a scoop the size of a paddling pool! To be honest with you, it was too much mash! We're only getting two chops, remember..."

Harry Hill

Two little girls are talking about how their parents make breakfast. "My mum's got a really cool toaster – when the toast is ready it beeps and a little light flashes." "That's nothing," says her friend, "When my dad makes the toast our toaster send out smoke signals."

Q: What sort of food decreases a woman's interest in sex dramatically?
A: Wedding cake.

A mum hosted a dinner party for the people from her work, all of whom were encouraged to bring their children along. All through the sit-down dinner one co-worker's little girl stared at one of the mums sitting across from her. The girl could hardly eat for staring. The woman checked her dress, felt her face for food, checked her hair was in place but nothing stopped the little girl from staring right across. She tried her best to just ignore the little girl but finally it was too much and she asked, "Why are you staring at me?" Everyone at the table had noticed the girl's behaviour so they all went quiet waiting for her response. The little girl said, "I'm just waiting to see you drink like a fish."

"Give a man a fish and he has food for a day; teach him how to fish and you can get rid of him of the entire weekend."
Zenna Schaffer

Benjamin comes home from school and asks his mum what there is for tea. "Enthusiasm stew," she says. "Enthusiasm stew?" he asks. "Why do you call it that?" "Because," says Mum, "I put everything I've got into it."

A little boy says to his mum, "Mum, the dinner lady said that eating spinach would put colour in my cheeks." "It seems to have worked," says his mum. "Now you've got a green face."

"When women are depressed, they eat or go shopping. Man invade another country. It's a whole different way of thinking."

Elayne Boolser

A young mum invites her ageing mother over for Sunday dinner. While she was in the kitchen preparing the meal, the old lady asked her grandson what they were having for dinner. "Goat," the little boy replied. "Goat?" replied the startled grandmother. "Is that right? Are you sure we're having goat?" "Yes," said the boy. "I heard my dad tell my mum, 'We might as well have the old goat for dinner today as any other day.'"

"The age of your children is a key factor in how quickly you are served in a restaurant. We once had a waiter in Canada who said, 'Could I get you your cheque?' and we answered, 'How about the menu first?'"

Erma Bombeck

Two kids tell their mum, "Mummy, it's Mother's Day today so you've got to stay in bed a bit longer." So Mum snuggles back down into bed and lies there, sniffing the lovely smell of bacon and eggs cooking downstairs and looking forward to being brought her breakfast in bed. A few minutes later, the children call her to come down where she finds them sitting at the table eating all the bacon and eggs. "See! Isn't this good," they say, "As a surprise for you for Mother's Day, we cooked breakfast for ourselves!"

"I have a nut allergy. When I was at school the other children used to make me play Russian Roulette by force-feeding me a packet of Revels."

Milton Jones

Cooking with mum

Ideal	Actual
Home-cooked food from recipes passed down through the generations	Warmed-up food passed down from yesterday's left-overs
Culinary delights conjured up as if by magic from the barest ingredients	Culinary curiosities dredged up with the barest of cookery skills
School lunchboxes filled with Mum's specialities	School lunchboxes filled with supermarket's special offers
Barbecues where Dad's allowed to take over	Barbecues where fire brigade is called to take over
Summer picnics with scrumptious home cooked delights and lashings of ginger beer	Summer picnics with flies and wasps and lashings of calamine lotion

Taking Food Safety A Bit Too Far

Only allowing the children organic bubble gum.

Sterilising your nipples with boiling water.

Not allowing baby to come into direct contact with your filthy un-sterilised nipples (which are a bit scabby and burnt from the attempts to sterilise them in boiling water anyway) so instead trying to use a water pistol-like-effect to squirt across a distance into his/her mouth – a bit like a Spaniard drinking wine.

Using an industrial belt-sander on fruit and vegetables before serving.

Demanding to inspect the kitchen before allowing children to have tea at a friend's house.

Refusing to buy food from any shop that also sells nuts.

Using a brand new unused solid silver cutlery set every mealtime and then throwing it away afterwards.

Why Dads And Kids Aren't Allowed In Kitchens

They don't know where anything is and therefore have to empty every single cupboard just to find the sugar.

Because even making a simple cup of tea will involve emptying said cupboards, leaving irremovable stains on the worktop and smashing at least one item of crockery.

Because they believe that kitchen knives also double as screwdrivers, saws, and impromptu sets of darts.

They don't realise that oven rings can be turned off as well as on.

They seem to think that the kitchen floor is also a sort of all-purpose workshop fit for stripping down motorbikes, oiling bicycles and building makeshift go-karts.

They contain dangerous things... called mothers.

They don't realise that the kitchen is a place for preparing food, they simply see it as a sort of stand-up serve yourself canteen.

Because it uses up the batteries in the smoke alarm too quickly.

Mum's Brownie Recipe

Here's a recipe to make Mum's famous brownies!

First of all pre-heat oven to gas mark six. Sniff air. Look in oven. Remove child's teddy bear from oven.

Melt eight ounces of margarine in a saucepan.

Sniff air again. Look in oven again. Remove teddy bear from oven again. Tell small child in kitchen, "Please don't do that."

Mix four ounces of sugar into margarine with wooden spoon.

Remove teddy bear from oven for a third time. Remove wooden spoon from child's mouth. Think about washing wooden spoon. Think what the hell, we're all family. Carry on mixing sugar, margarine and child's saliva with wooden spoon.

Reach for cocoa powder. Ask child where he has put cocoa powder. Notice your white cat is now a brown cat.

Clean cuts and scratches sustained while trying to wash cocoa powder out of cat's fur and apply antiseptic and bandages.

Use hand mixer to mix four eggs, eight ounces of sifted flour and two teaspoons of vanilla essence.

Sniff air. Remove teddy from oven again. Then clean egg, flour and vanilla essence off child, walls, ceiling, kitchen surfaces and cat.

Sniff air. Remove teddy. Open doors and windows for ventilation and remove batteries from kitchen smoke alarm.

Add four ounces of nuts and pinch of salt and beat all ingredients together. Pick out any visible cat hairs from mixture.

Let cat out of fridge.

Pour mixture into a well greased baking tray. Bake for 25 minutes.

Make icing with eight ounces of sugar, four ounces of

margarine and one ounce of chocolate. Remove the f.....lipping teddy bear from the flipping saucepan and throw it far far away.

Notice ringing sound, check batteries are still out of smoke alarm, realize it's the door bell. Answer door and discover it is a nice policeman returning child who had wandered into busy street to retrieve charred teddy bear.

Put child in back garden.

Add two fluid ounces of milk and stir.

Answer door and spend several minutes apologizing to neighbour for child having used hose to play target practice with his garden gnomes.

Attach child to washing line. Sniff air. Remember you were making brownies. Remove smouldering ruins from oven and serve.

Advice From Kids On Romantic Issues

"Just see if the man picks up the cheque. That's how you can tell if he's in love."

Nine-year-old boy (on how to tell if two people having dinner together in a restaurant are in love)

"Lovers will just be staring at each other and their food will get cold. Other people care more about the food."

Eight-year-old boy (on how to tell if two people having dinner together in a restaurant are in love)

"It's love if they order one of those desserts that are on fire. They like to order those because it's just like how their hearts are... on fire."

Nine-year-old girl (on how to tell if two people having dinner together in a restaurant are in love)

The Toddler Diet...

So, Mum, worried about packing on the pounds after giving birth? Well, why not try eating the same way your toddler does...

Day one:

Breakfast - One scrambled egg and one piece of toast with strawberry jam. Eat two bites of scrambled egg using your fingers, then stick some up your nose and dump the rest on the floor, thereby avoiding a lot of unnecessary calories. Pick up toast, then just before it reaches your mouth, smear the lot all over your face. End meal with a vigorous aerobic screaming fit.

Lunch - Four crayons (choose various bright colours to make sure you're getting a full range of different vitamins). End meal with another vigorous aerobic screaming fit.

Dinner – Eat a jar of baby food being very careful the whole time that you don't swallow any of it. During the course of the meal try to reach a point where you have the entire contents of the jar wobbling precariously on your lower lip before letting it drop on floor and/or on cat's head.

Day two:

Breakfast - Pick up last night's dinner from kitchen floor and eat it along with contents of cat's bowl. Enjoy a few minutes vigorous work-out into nappy.

Lunch – Take bowl of baby food and, using spoon, re-decorate walls and ceiling of kitchen with it.

Afternoon Snack – For a bit of roughage, take dummy into garden and drop in soil. Retrieve and slurp until it is clean again. For some extra fibre, bring dummy back inside, drop on rug, pick up and slurp again.

Dinner – There should be plenty of leftovers to be used up by now. You'll find them in the grooves and on the underside of the table on your high chair and they should be nice and chewy.

Final day:

Breakfast – Make sure you have plenty of meat-based protein by eating at least five plastic farm animals. For a special pudding afterwards, treat yourself to a box of apple pies (that's obviously the cardboard box itself rather than the apple pies it contained, which should be force fed to cat).

Lunch – For some fruit, eat a cherry lip gloss. End meal with cigarette – that's to eat rather than to smoke, of course.

Dinner – Just to make sure you really aren't putting on any weight whatsoever, bring up everything consumed in past three days.

Glossary of Kids' Kitchen Terms

Appetizing: Anything advertised on TV.

Boil: The point a parent reaches upon hearing the automatic "Yuck" before a food is even tasted.

Casserole: Combination of favourite foods that go uneaten because they are mixed together.

Chair: Spot left vacant by mid-meal bathroom visit.

Cookie (Last One): Item that must be eaten in front of a sibling.

Crust: Part of a sandwich saved for the starving children of [ ] China, [ ] India, [ ] Africa or [ ] Middle-East (check one).

Desserts: The reason for eating a meal.

Evaporate: Magic trick performed by children when it comes time to clear the table or wash dishes.

Fat: Microscopic substance detected visually by children on pieces of meat they do not wish to eat.

Floor: Place for all food not found on lap or chair.

Fork: Eating utensil made obsolete by discovery of fingers.

Fried Foods: Gourmet cooking.

Frozen: Condition of children's jaws when spinach is served.

Fruit: A natural sweet not to be confused with dessert.

Germs: The only thing kids will share freely.

Kitchen: The only room not used when eating crumbly snacks.

Leftovers: Commonly described as "gross".

Liver: A food that affects genes, creating a hereditary dislike.

Lollipop: A snack provided by people who don't have to pay dental bills.

Macaroni: Material for a collage.

Measuring Cup: A kitchen utensil usually stored in the sandbox.

Metric: A system of measurement that will be accepted only after 40 years of wandering in the desert.

Napkin: Any warm cloth object, such as shirt or pants.

Natural Food: Food eaten with unwashed hands.

Nutrition: Secret war waged by parents using direct commands, camouflage, and constant guard duty.

Plate: A breakable Frisbee.

Refrigerator: A very expensive and inefficient room air conditioner when not being used as an art gallery.

Saliva: A medium for blowing bubbles.

Canned drink: Shake 'n' Spray.

Table: A place for storing chewing gum.

Table Leg: Percussion instrument.

Thirsty: How your child feels after you've said your final "good night".

Vegetable: A basic food known to satisfy kid's hunger – but only by sight.

Water: The cola of underdeveloped countries.

You Know You're A Mum When...

- You refer to your husband as "Dad", and your mum as "Grandma".
- You can't face dinner because you've been eating the kids' leftovers at their tea time.
- You get excited when a big new children's film comes out.
- You only ever buy cereal that has marshmallows in it.
- The closest you get to gourmet cooking is making Rice Crispie bars.
- You think five consecutive hours of sleep is a restful night.
- The pockets of every coat you own are filled with cereal.
- You see an old picture of yourself and you remember having a life of your own.
- The chance of a night out is savoured for weeks beforehand.
- All of a sudden dad has to keep "working late".
- You never take a vacation without your in-laws.

- You begin to view your Disney characters as your friends – or is that vice-versa?
- You actually do grow eyes in the back of your head.
- You find yourself speaking to your partner in short, breathy commands "Milk, now!" or "I want juuuuuuuuice!"
- You don't think you sound ridiculous when you say, "Little Johnny, stop licking the framed poster of Gustav Klimt's 'The Kiss'!"
- A special offer at the supermarket is your highlight of the week (especially when it's buy one get one free bottles of wine).
- You find yourself saying things your mum used to say to you.
- Nothing surprises you anymore.

Do The Mum: A Guide To Doing All Those Funny Little Dances Mums Can't Help Themselves From Going Into At Family Parties, Discos, Weddings etc

The imaginary plate spin

This involves holding both index fingers above head and twirling in tiny circles as if spinning imaginary dinner plates – sometimes accompanied by a fairly feeble and unconvincing "whoo!" noise.

The aerobic workout

As Mum's exercise routine and figure have been severely compromised by the arrival of children this is an opportunistic attempt to make the most of any excuse to fling her limbs about with abandon. Other dancers beware!

The imaginary boat row

Mums of a certain age, after a certain amount of alcohol consumption will sit on the floor in a line and row an imaginary boat – though nobody knows quite why.

The unfunky chicken

This involves strutting up and down the dancefloor and pumping elbows on and off one's sides in a sort of demented chicken impersonation.

The Leo Sayer finger dance

Minimal involvement from the leg department but incorporating extended index fingers pointing (pointlessly) at ceiling. Possibly a Freudian indication that said mum wishes she was fast a-kip in her bed.

You Might Be A Clinging Mum If...

- Your child's primary school children has permanently assigned you your own chair, desk and coat peg as well as adding your name to the class register.
- Instead of letting your child go out and play with other children in the road you make them watch through the window while you go out and play with them instead.
- You apply to do a degree as a mature student so you can be with your child at university.
- You insist on sitting in the back of the car with them – even when you're driving.
- You have your emergency contact details tattooed onto them.
- You've pasted a picture of yourself into the lid of their school lunch box so they won't forget you.

- After your husband has given your daughter away as a bride, you ask for her back.
- You carry on walking your child to school... even though they're now working there as a teacher.

Advice From Kids On Romantic Issues

"No person really decides before they grow up who they're going to marry. God decides it all way before, and you get to find out later who you're stuck with."

Ten-year-old girl (on marriage)

"Married people usually look happy to talk to other people."

Boy aged six (on how you can tell if two people are married or not)

"You might have to guess, based on whether they seem to be yelling at the same kids."

Eight-year-old boy (on how you can tell if two people are married or not)

"One of you should know how to write a cheque. Because, even if you have tons of love, there is still going to be a lot of bills."

Girl aged eight (on how to choose who you should get married to)

"When somebody's been dating for a while, the boy might propose to the girl. He says to her, 'I'll take you for a whole life, or at least until we have kids and get divorced.'"

Girl aged nine (on marriage proposals)

"A man and a woman promise to go through sickness and illness and diseases together."

Boy aged ten (on getting married)

All You Need To Know About Mothers As Told By Primary School Children

Why did God give you to your mother and not some other mum?
We're related.
God knew she likes me a lot more than other people's mums like me.

What kind of little girl was your mum?
My mum has always been my mum and none of that other stuff.
I don't know because I wasn't there, but my guess would be pretty bossy.
They say she used to be nice.

How did your mum meet your dad?
Mum was working in a store and Dad was shoplifting.

Mums and Dads

Mum and dad are a team right? Hmm. Now what sort of team is this when the team leader does all the work, and the rest of the team is on the touchline shouting the occasional bit of encouragement before going down the pub? But let's not be too hard on the dads; some of them do their fair share, they do their bit (bit being the operative word). For example, Mum does the washing and ironing, and Dad arranges his dirty clothes in a handy pile on the bedroom floor. Mum does the shopping and cooking, and Dad eats the stuff. You can't say he's not contributing, ladies! And as for rearing children, Dad was there at the conception, and probably the birth too. He probably thinks that any other contribution he makes is just the icing on the cake.

"Mothers are a biological necessity; fathers are a social invention."

Margaret Mead

A mum goes to the doctors and is asked by him if there is any insanity in the family. "Oh yes, definitely," says the mum. "My husband has these delusions that he's in charge in our house."

My mother was a ventriloquist. She always was throwing her voice. For ten years I thought the dog was telling me to kill my father.

"Mothers are fonder than fathers of their children because they are more certain they are their own."

Aristotle

A little girl asks her mummy, "Do all fairy tales begin 'Once upon a time'?" "No," says Mummy. "Your daddy's usually begin, 'The train was late again...'"

You know when you've asked Mum a really good question because she says, "Ask your father!"

And if it's a really really good question he says, "Ask your mother!"

"Mom and Pop were just a couple of kids when they got married. He was 18, she was 16, and I was three."

Billie Holiday

"Men name their children after themselves, women don't. Have you ever met a Sally Junior?"

Rita Rudner

My mum and dad are cousins, which explains why I look so much like myself.

Dad is in the kitchen making tea one day, when Mum walks in. "Oh no, no, no!" she says when she sees him. "What the hell do you think you're doing? You haven't put the milk in before the tea bag have you? Are you sure the water's boiled? Have you remembered to put the sugar in? Mind you don't slop the tea all over the cup when your stir it! Good God, it's simple enough isn't it?" "What on earth are you doing," asks Dad. "Don't you think I know how to make a cup of tea?" "Yes," says Mum. "But I just thought you'd like to know how it feels to have you sitting next to me when I'm driving."

"I never married, because there was no need. I have three pets at home which answer the same purpose as a husband. I have a dog that growls every morning, a parrot that swears all afternoon, and a cat that comes home late every night."

Marie Corelli

Bill and Jane are a couple having trouble getting their new home computer up and running. In the end, there's nothing for it and they phone the computer company's help desk for advice. Unfortunately the help desk proves not to be completely helpful as the person on the other end of the line speaks entirely in computer jargon. "Look, sorry," says Bill, "I'm not able to follow any of this. Could you just tell me what to do as if I were a four-year-old." "OK," says the help desk technician. "Sonny, could you go and get your mummy on the line to speak to me?"

Shanice comes home proudly from a disco one evening and announces to her mother, "Mum, I've found a man just like Daddy." "Well," says Mum, "You'll get no sympathy from me, young lady."

> **"Whatever women must do they must do twice as well as men to be thought half as good. Luckily, this is not difficult."**
>
> **Charlotte Whitton**

One afternoon a man comes home from work and finds total mayhem in his house. His three children are outside, still dressed in their pyjamas and playing in the mud with empty food boxes and wrappers strewn all around the front yard. The door of his wife's car is open and so is the front door to the house. Inside he finds an even bigger mess. A lamp has been knocked over and the throw rug is wadded against one wall. In the front room the TV is blaring away and the floor in the back room is covered with toys and bits of clothing. In the kitchen the sink is full of dishes, breakfast is spilled all over the work surfaces, the fridge door is open wide, there's dog food all over the floor, a broken glass under the table, and a small pile of sand by the back door. He goes up the stairs, stepping over toys and more piles of clothes, looking for his wife. Perhaps she's ill or something even more serious has happened? He finds a trickle of water making its way out of the bathroom door. Inside he finds wet towels, scummy soap and more toys strewn over the floor. Miles of toilet paper lie in a heap and toothpaste has been smeared over the mirror and walls. He rushes to the bedroom and finds his wife curled up in bed. He looks at her in bewilderment and asks, "What the hell happened here today?" She smiles and answers, "Well, you know every other day when you come home from work you always ask me what on earth have I been doing all day?" "Yes," he says. "Well," she replies, "today I didn't do it."

A man comes home from the pub pushing a baby carriage. "You stupid idiot!" says his wife. "That's not our baby!" "I know," says the husband. "But it's a nicer pram isn't it?"

Two mums are talking. My husband's such a whinger," says the first. "When I came home the other day he that the cat had upset him." "What did you say?" asks the second. "I told him he shouldn't have eaten it in the first place."

Dad wakes up with a terrible hangover. He yawns, scratches himself, opens his eyes and sees a glass of water and some aspirins next to the bed on the table. He takes them and then notices his clothes on the chair all clean and pressed. He looks around the room and notices everything is neat and tidy. He gets dressed, then he sees a note propped up by the mirror which reads: "Good morning darling, breakfast is on the table, coffee's in the pot. Enjoy! Love you." He goes downstairs and sees his daughter at the breakfast table where his breakfast is ready and waiting with the newspaper open at the sports page. He rubs his eyes and asks his daughter what had happened the night before. "Well," she says, "You rolled in about half past three roaring drunk. You tripped over the cat, broke Mum's favourite vase, threw up in the umbrella stand, and fell asleep on the kitchen floor." "So, why has Mum done all this for me then?" he asks, totally confused. "Everything neat and tidy, aspirins, clean clothes, breakfast, newspaper, coffee..." "Ah!" says his daughter, "Well you see, Mum managed to get you upstairs to the bedroom, and when she tried to take your trousers off you shouted, "How dare you, madam! Get your hands off me, you hussy! I'm married!"

"My mother buried three husbands, and two of them were just napping."

Rita Rudner

Mum decided that now Jake was four he ought to learn to start putting his clothes in the washing basket when they were dirty. As usual he took off his dirty clothes and waited for Mum to pick them up. "Now Jake," said Mum, "I want you to take your dirty clothes and go and put them where we're supposed when they're dirty." So little Jake dutifully picked up his dirty clothes and put them on the floor on Dad's side of the bed.

A woman with a new-born baby marches into the local baker's shop and says to the owner "See this baby! It's yours – now tell me what the hell are you going to do about it?" The baker asks her to keep her voice down and says, "Look, I'll tell you what. I'll give you fresh bread, rolls and cakes every day for the next five years if you'll just keep quiet about the whole thing." "OK," says the woman, "but you better make sure the deliveries keep coming until he's 16, or I'll tell your wife." "All right, all right," says the baker, "Anything you say." So for the next 16 years the baker is as good as his word and delivers fresh bread, rolls, and cakes to the woman and her child. Finally, when the boy is 16 the baker arrives with the very last bag of goodies. "There you are," he says, handing the bag over to the now 16-year-old boy, "That's the last lot. Pity your mother isn't here. I'd like to see the look on her face when she realizes she won't be getting any more freebies out of me." "Well," says the boy, "It is a pity she isn't here, because I know she wanted to see the look on your face when you found out about all the stuff she's been getting for the past 16 years from the butcher, the greengrocer, the milkman and the coalman."

"The place of the father in the modern suburban family is a very small one, particularly if he plays golf."

Bertrand Russell

Mum is getting little Chesney ready to go to a fifth birthday party, and she's trying to explain that he must be very grown up and show good manners. "Now dear," she says, "If you're offered seconds of anything, just say no politely, just as Daddy does." When Chesney gets home with his party bag and balloon, his mother asks if he had a nice time and whether he remembered to behave as she'd asked him to. "Oh yes," replied Chesney, "I had my first piece of birthday cake, and then Mrs Jones asked if I'd like a second piece. "And you answered just as Daddy would did you?" asked Mum. "Yes," said Chesney, "I said "No way, I'm not eating any more of that crap!"

When my mum was trying to cut down on food I helped her by attaching a picture of a beautiful slim model to the front of the fridge. It worked! My mum lost 18 pounds. The only problem was my dad put on three stone!

> **"I have yet to hear a man ask for advice on how to combine marriage and a career."**
> **Gloria Steinem**

A brand-new shopping centre was opened where a woman could choose a husband. There were five floors in the building and as the women went up to each floor they found the men increasing in positive attributes. The only rule was that if you didn't choose a man from one floor and you went up to find a better one you couldn't go back down except to leave the place. A group of women decided to go and check the place out. On the first floor was a sign saying: "Every one of these men has a job and loves children." The women read the sign and said "Well that's pretty good for starters, but things can only get better if we go up to the next floor. Let's go and have a look." On the second floor was another sign saying: "Every one of these men has a fabulous salary, loves children and is very handsome." The women are very impressed, but their curiosity gets the better of them and they decide to go up another level. On the third floor was another sign saying: "Every one of these men has a fabulous salary, loves children, is very handsome and does his share of the housework." At this point the women start to waver and wonder whether they should choose a husband there and then, but they then remember that things should be even better on the next floor and go up expectantly. On the fourth floor was another sign saying: "Every one of these men has a fabulous salary, loves children, is very handsome, does his share of the housework and is very, very romantic." "Wow!" say the women, "they sound almost too good to be true, but hey, we've got one more floor to go, let's go and find out what's up there." So off they troop, full of anticipation. And there on the top floor was just one sign saying: "For goodness sake, you women are just impossible to please. Thank you for shopping and have a nice day!"

One the first day of school the teacher is getting acquainted with her new pupils and asking about their families. She turns to one little boy and says "Now Nathan, what does your daddy do?" "Whatever my mum tells him," says Nathan.

A judge is presiding over a rather acrimonious divorce and the couple are making an issue of every single thing they can. When it comes to who should get custody of their only child the father says he thinks she should stay with him as the mother is irresponsible. The mother says to the judge that as she brought her daughter into the world she should get custody. The judge asks the husband if he has any argument against this. The husband thinks for a moment and replies, "Well Your Honour, if you put five pounds into a cigarette machine, would the cigarettes belong to you or the machine?"

> **"A man's got to do what a man's got to do. A woman must do what he can't."**
>
> **Rhonda Hansome**

Little boy: "My dad says he always takes my mum to the finest restaurants, and one day he might even let her inside one."

Mum one: "My husband's so tight fisted. This year he didn't bother hiding any Easter eggs for the children." Mum two: "Why not?" Mum one: "He said they still hadn't found the ones he hid last year."

One morning a little girl bursts into the kitchen at her house and tells her parents, "Dad! Mum! I have some great news for you! I am getting married to the greatest hunk in the world. He lives in the biggest house in the best part of town and his name is Jeff." After dinner, Dad takes the daughter aside and tells her. "Honey, I have to talk with you. Your mother and I have been married a long time. She's a wonderful wife but she's never offered much excitement in the bedroom. I have fooled around with other women a lot. I'm sorry. This Jeff you've fallen for is actually your half-brother, and I'm afraid you can't marry him." The girl is heartbroken, but after eight months she eventually starts dating again. A year later she comes home and very proudly announces, “Mitch asked me to marry him! We’re getting married in June.” Again her father takes her aside and breaks the sad news. “Mitch is your half-brother too. I’m terribly sorry about this.” The girl is furious! She finally decided to go to her mother and tell her. “Dad has done so much harm. I guess I’m never going to get married,” she complained. “Every time I fall in love, Dad tells me the guy is my half-brother.” Her mum just shakes her head and says, “Don’t you pay any attention to what he says, dear. He’s not your father.

Approaches To Dealing With Problem Behaviour From Partner

Withholding beer money

This can be tricky if your partner is the main breadwinner in the house, but if you tell him that the only way you can keep on top of the household budget is by having total control over all funds. You are then well on the way to granting him a bit of pocket money each week, which can be withheld when he steps out of line.

Grounding him

Again, not so easy as when dealing with a child, but as you are in complete control of all washing and ironing duties it is but a simple manoeuvre to tell him everything’s in the wash just as he’s getting ready to go out.

Pretending to be mortified at his bad behaviour

And let’s face it girls, do you really need to pretend that much?

Make him sit on his own special naughty step

The naughty step idea can surely be adapted to be used on your child's father. Eventually you might be able to get the whole family sitting around the place on their own individual naughty steps and looking like a team of performing seals.

If your partner is of a DIY-bent you can get him to build his own naughty step out of a bit of plywood. There will then be no stopping him and before you know it he will have embellished it with a little bookshelf, shoe holder and pipe rack.

Deny him things that he enjoys until he starts behaving himself

This is such an easy one, as there's one obvious thing that he enjoys that you can deny him. Many mothers take this policy to an extreme however, and the thing that's being denied remains witheld for the entire period of child rearing. Just make sure not to give him the chance to go look for it elsewhere (see grounding).

Use distraction techniques

Male partners are much more easily distracted than children. In fact it could be argued that men's lives are spent in a near permanent state of distraction with the thing they're actually meant to be focussing on at any given moment never being entirely clear. The mere mention of words such as "football", "beer", "cars" or "sex" is often quite sufficient to distract them utterly from any errant behaviour.

Pretend to encounter some slight difficulty while doing something

This is a fail-safe way of diverting your male partner from his problem behaviour. Simply act as though you're encountering some minor problem with what you're doing. This might be making the dinner, changing a nappy or re-decorating the spare bedroom. The man will then be immediately cease his problem behaviour and will instead spend the rest of the evening showing you exactly how you should have gone about doing what you were trying to do while tutting and muttering to himself.

Children's Books We'll Probably Never See

Strangers Have All The Best Sweeties
The Little Sissy Who Snitched
Some Kittens Can Fly!
Getting More Chocolate on Your Face
Where Would You Like to Be Buried?
Kathy Was So Bad Her Mummy Stopped Loving Her
The Attention Deficit Disorder Association's Book of Wild Animals of Western Eur – Hey! Let's Go And Play On The X-Box!
All Dogs Go to Hell
The Kids' Guide to Hitchhiking
You Are Different and That's Bad
Dad's New Wife Lawrence
Pop! Goes the Hamster... and Other Great Microwave Games
Testing Homemade Parachutes Using Only Your Household Pets
The Hardy Boys, the Barbie Twins, and the Vice Squad
Babar Meets the Taxidermist
Curious George and the High-Voltage Fence
The Boy Who Died from Eating All His Vegetables
Start Your Own Housing Empire with the Change from Your Mum's Purse
The Pop-up Book of Human Anatomy
Things Rich Kids Have That You'll Never Even Touch
The Care Bears Maul Some Campers and Are Shot Dead
How to Become the Dominant Military Power in Your Primary School
Controlling the Playground: Respect through Fear
When Mummy and Daddy Don't Know the Answer, They Say God Did It
Garfield Gets Feline Leukaemia
What Is That Dog Doing to That Other Dog?
Why Can't Mr. Fork and Ms. Electrical Outlet Be Friends?
Bi-Curious George
Daddy Drinks Because You Cry
You Were an Accident

All You Need To Know About Mothers As Told By Primary School Children

What did your mum need to know about your dad before she married him?

His last name.
She had to know his background. Like is he a crook?
Does he get drunk on beer? Does he make at least £800 a year?
Did he say NO to drugs and YES to chores?

Why did your mum marry your dad?

My dad makes the best spaghetti in the world. And my mum eats a lot.
She got too old to do anything else with him.
My grandma says that Mum didn't have her thinking cap on.

Who's the boss at your house?

Mum doesn't want to be boss, but she has to because Dad's such a goofball.
Mum. You can tell by room inspection. She sees the stuff under the bed.
I guess Mum is, but only because she has a lot more to do than Dad.

What's the difference between mums and dads?

Mums work at work and work at home, and dads just go to work at work.
Mums know how to talk to teachers without scaring them.
Dads are taller and stronger, but mums have all the real power 'cause that's who you've got to ask if you want to sleep over at your friend's.

How Men And Women Divide The Parenting Duties

When a child asks for something a bit out of the ordinary, Mum says "Ask your dad", and Dad of course says "Ask your mum" – after a few rounds of this the child forgets what the original question was. Problem solved!

Dad plays at pirates, cowboys, and soldiers. Mum plays at nurses – especially after dad's had a particularly rough time playing pirates, cowboys and soldiers.

Dad gets the kids to help him wash the car, Mum cleans and dries the kids after they've helped Daddy wash the car.

Dad takes the kids on a countryside walk, collecting sticks, stones and leaves along the way. Mum teaches the kids recycling by chucking these found objects in the bin.

Dad shows his son how to take apart a motorbike engine on the kitchen floor. Mum shows his son how to take Dad apart on the kitchen floor.

When his child misbehaves badly, Mum says "You wait till your father gets home." When Dad gets home he shouts at the child then Mum gives the child a cuddle and protects him from nasty Dad.

If anything of a mechanical nature is to be operated Dad is expected to be able to deal with it – with the honourable exceptions of the washing machine, tumble drier, dishwasher, vacuum cleaner, cooker, fridge, freezer, iron, food mixer and toaster – which are of course Mum's area of expertise.

Dad is expected to do DIY jobs around the house. Mum is expected to rush him to casualty afterwards.

Mum is the sympathetic ear, the comforting arms, and the calming voice – she is expected to use these with the children as well.

It's Mum's job to remember the birthdays, anniversaries, and other significant dates of every member of the family and the extended family. It's Dad's job to remember Mum's birthday and his own wedding anniversary – and he still forgets!

How Mums And Dads Are Role Models

Boys learn from their dads that men make all the important decisions in the house; girls learn from their mums that they have to let men think they've made all the important decisions in the house.

Boys learn from their dads that men are the breadwinners; girls learn from their mums that left to their own devices men wouldn't have the first idea where to buy bread, or how much to pay for it.

Boys learn from their dads that they shouldn't cry when they hurt themselves; girls learn from their mums how to come up with increasingly inventive and amusing ways to hurt men.

Boys learn from their dads that all other road users are idiots; girls learn from their mums that all those idiotic road users are men.

Boys learn from their dads how to hold their drink; girls learn from their mums that they if they play their cards right they'll never need to buy a drink in their lives.

Boys learn from their dads that men should look manly; girls learn from their mums that it's the women who wear the trousers.

Boys learn from their dads which football team to support; girls learn from their mums that Saturday afternoon is a good time to borrow dad's credit card.

Boys learn from their dads that a little lady likes nothing better than to end up with a ring on her finger; girls learn from their mums that the main thing girls can get wrapped round their finger is a man.

Boys learn from their dads that women are the weaker sex; girls learn from their mums that you've got to let men think what they want as long as you're getting your own way.

Boys learn from their dads that they are God's gift to women; girls learn from their mums to hang on to their receipt in case they need to take him back and exchange him.

How Mums Are Different From Dads

Mum getting you dressed:
Carefully selecting crisp, clean, ironed clothes from wardrobe.

Dad getting you dressed:
Finding whatever's on bedroom floor from day before, giving it all a quick sniff and "that'll do you another day, son!"

Mum cooking dinner:
Remembering everyone's likes, dislikes, requirements and allergies.

Dad cooking dinner:
Only remembering something's cooking when smoke alarm goes off.

Mum buying a present:
Spending several hours in careful consideration before choosing the perfect thing that the recipient might well have chosen for themselves.

Dad buying a present:
Choosing just the first thing he sees which he would like and which he then assumes that anyone else in their right mind would like too.

Mum asking what you did at school today:
Remembering the names and allegiances of all your friends, teachers and classmates and taking a keen interest.

Dad asking what you did at school today:
"Anything happen at school, son? Nothing? OK."

Mum saying goodbye at school:
A big hug, a big kiss and standing at the school gates waving for half the morning.

Dad saying goodbye at school:
A quick ruffle of the hair and a shove out of the car door before tyres screech and child is left in a small dense cloud of exhaust fumes.

Mum writing a sick note to school:
"Please excuse him from PE today as he has had a poorly tummy."

Dad writing a sick note to school:
"The lad has had the trots all night and so does not need to do PE today."

Mum watching you play a football match:
Cheering you on regardless of the score.

Dad watching you play a football match:
Swearing at the referee, getting extremely upset then telling you all the way home how you could have won it and beginning to wonder if this really is his natural offspring.

Mum comforting you after a fall:
"Oh dear me! Who's a brave little soldier?"

Dad comforting you after a fall:
"Stop that blubbing or I'll really give you something to cry about!"

Mum's Best Jokes About Men

Q: Why are men like miniskirts?
A: If you're not careful, they'll creep right up your legs.

Q: Why are men like holidays?
A: They never seem to last as long as you want.

Q: Why are men like blenders?
A: You feel you need to get yourself one, but you're never quite sure why.

Q: Why are men like popcorn?
A: They will satisfy you, but not for that long.

Q: Why are men are like sink plungers?
A: They spend all of their time in one of two places: the DIY shop or the bathroom.

Q: Why are men like bank accounts?
A: Without a lot of money, they don't generate much interest.

Q: Why are men like mascara?
A: They usually run at the first sign of emotion.

Q: Why are men like animals?
A: They're messy, they're insensitive and they're potentially violent – but on the plus side they do make quite good pets.

Q: Why are men like lava lamps?
A: They're good fun to watch, but they're not really that bright.

Q: Why are men like horoscopes?
A: They're always telling you what you should do, and they are always wrong.

Q: Why are men like parking spaces?
A: The good ones have all been taken and the rest are handicapped.

Q: Why are men like chocolate bars?
A: They're sweet, smooth but they usually head straight for your hips.

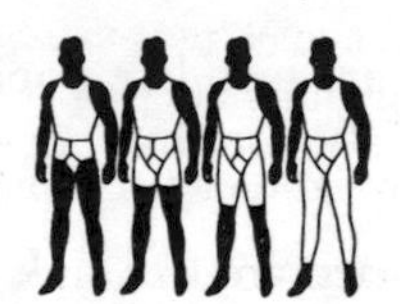

A Guide To Mum's Old Boyfriends

Dopey but dependable – He was never going to stray, but that's mainly because he'd never have had the opportunity. Probable name: Brian

Unreliable ladies' man – Mum couldn't possibly have married him because he would have been snogging one of the bridesmaids at the reception. Probable name: Vince

Mr Sporty – Could never have arranged a marriage as weddings are usually on a Saturday and that's football day innit? Probable name: Shane

Mr Nerdy – Lovely chap, but his idea of a weekend away was visiting a bus ticket museum in Arbroathshire. Probable name: Nigel

The grease monkey – Big motorbike and shiny leathers, but unfortunately he spent most of his time tinkering with the engine, or waxing the chrome. Probable name: Steve

The Objects On Mum's Desk At Work

Picture of the kids in school uniform to remind you a) what they look like, and b) why you had to go back to work in the first place.

Clay model of Dad you can stick pins in when he phones to say he can't collect kids from school after all.

Misshapen plaster paperweight made by one of your children.

Picture of Brad Pitt to remind you of days when you still thought you were in with a chance.

List of things to do when you get home, and things to buy on the way.

Nintendo DS Tamagotchi that's she's been instructed to feed and look after while child is at school.

Mug emblazoned with "I love Mum" from last Mothers' Day.

Three month old home-made birthday cards that she can't bear to throw away.

Top Tips To Get Dad Helping Round The House

Tell him your house has been picked for a reality TV show and it needs to be in shape before the production crew arrives.

Burn holes in his best shirts and he'll volunteer to iron them himself next time.

Hire a beautiful young au pair and he'll suddenly be very to keen to help her with the washing up.

Ask him if he'd like a fabulous new state-of-the-art piece of technological kit for his birthday and buy him his own washing machine.

Pretend that you've invited his boss over for dinner and say you'll be so busy preparing food that he'll have to get the place tidied up.

Ways For Mums To Give Kids Incentives

Keep your room tidy and I'll continue to provide meals.

If you behave you might reach your next birthday.

Keeping back a few Christmas presents to be released at intervals dependent on good behaviour.

If you don't eat it up right now I'll let Dad cook your next meal.

Do well in your exams and you won't have to clean your own house when you grow up like I do.

If you pass your GCSEs we'll buy you a brand new bike, and if you pass your A levels we'll get you a saddle to go with it.

Mum's Survival Tips

Don't sweat your every mistake or faux pas. They make up for the things you got away with that nobody knows about.

Avoid marrying anyone who deliberately flushes the toilet when you're taking a shower.

When someone tells you that what he's about to say is "for your own good", expect the worst.

The value of a dog is its constant reminder of how much fun it is to act idiotic.

If you are lavishly praised, enjoy the taste but don't swallow it whole.

When a politician says "Let me make something perfectly clear", remember that he usually won't.

You children may leave home, but their stuff will be in your attic and basement forever.

If someone says, "I know what I mean, but I just can't put it into words", he doesn't know what he means.

Two people cannot operate a TV remote control in the same room at the same time.

Murphy's Laws For Mums

Any item of children's clothing that you find you have no choice but to buy today will be in a half price sale in one week's time.

Drink bottles that advertise themselves as being "leak proof" probably aren't.

The chances of a piece of bread falling with the blackcurrant jam side down are directly proportional to the cost of the carpet.

The bin lorry will be two doors past your house when the argument over whose day it is to take out the rubbish this week and anyway is it the blue bin or the green bin or the brown bin that you have to put out this week this week finally ends.

The shirt your child has to wear today will be the only one that is in the laundry basket with a massive horrible stain all over the front of it.

Gym clothes left at school in lockers get covered in mildew at a faster rate than any other clothing even if it is left out in a swamp.

The item your child has lost, and must have for school within the next ten seconds, will be found in the last place you look five minutes after you gave up and sent them to school without it.

Sick children recover miraculously as soon as you walk them into the doctor's surgery.

Refrigerated items, used daily, will make their way to the back of the fridge.

Your chances of being seen by someone you know dramatically increase if you drive your child to school in your dressing gown and pyjamas.

Genuine Extracts From Teenagers' Exam Answers and Essays That Should Make Their Mums Proud

The theory of evolution was greatly objected to because it made man think.

Three kinds of blood vessels are arteries, vanes and caterpillars.

The process of turning steam back into water again is called conversation.

The Earth makes one resolution every 24 hours.

To collect fumes of sulphur, hold a deacon over a flame in a test tube.

Algebraical symbols are used when you do not know what you are talking about.

The pistol of a flower is its only protection against insects.

Dew is formed on leaves when the sun shines down on them and makes them perspire.

A super-saturated solution is one that holds more than it can hold.

A triangle which has an angle of 135 degrees is called an obscene triangle.

When you haven't got enough iodine in your blood you get a glacier.

When you smell an odourless gas, it is probably carbon monoxide.

Many dead animals of the past changed to fossils, while others preferred to be oil.

All animals were here before mankind. The animals lived peacefully until mankind came along and made roads, houses, hotels and condoms.

The largest mammals are to be found in the sea because there is nowhere else to put them.

Methane, a greenhouse gas, comes from the burning of trees and cows.

The spinal column is a long bunch of bones. The head sits on the top and you sit on the bottom.

Mushrooms always grow in damp places and so they look like umbrellas.

Most books say the sun is a star. But it still knows how to change back into the sun in the daytime.

Cadavers are dead bodies that have donated themselves to science.

Parallel lines never meet unless you bend one or both of them.

A circle is a figure with 0 corners and only one side.

Genetics explains why you look like your father and if you don't, why you should.

If conditions are not favourable, bacteria go into a period of adolescence.

When oxygen is combined with anything, heat is given off. This is known as constipation.

You can listen to thunder after lightning and tell how close you came to getting hit. If you don't hear it, you got hit, so never mind.

The body consists of three parts - the branium, the borax, and the abominable cavity. The branium contains the brain, the borax contains the heart and lungs, and the abominable cavity contains the bowels, of which there are five - a, e, i, o, and u.

Water is composed of two gins, Oxygin and Hydrogin. Oxygin is pure gin. Hydrogin is gin and water.

Blood flows down one leg and up the other.

Respiration is composed of two acts, first inspiration, and then expectoration.

The moon is a planet just like the earth, only it is even deader.

Artificial insemination is when the farmer does it to the cow instead of the bull.

The skeleton is what is left after the insides have been taken out and the outsides have been taken off.

The tides are a fight between the Earth and moon. All water tends towards the moon, because there is no water in the moon, and nature abhors a vacuum. I forget where the sun joins in this fight.

More Genuine Extracts From Teenagers' Exam Papers and Essays Which Their Mums Should Be Proud Of

Q: What is a fossil?
A: A fossil is an extinct animal. The older it is, the more extinct it is.

Q: What is the meaning of the word Germinate?
A: To become a naturalized German.

Q: What is a magnet?
A: Something you find crawling all over a dead cat.

Q: Define momentum.
A: What you give a person when they are going away.

Q: What is the definition of a planet?
A: A body of Earth surrounded by sky.

Q: What is rhubarb?
A: A kind of celery gone bloodshot.

Q: Define a vacuum.
A: It's a large, empty space where the pope lives.

Q: How do you keep milk from turning sour?
A: Keep it in the cow.

Q: Who was Charles Darwin?
A: Charles Darwin was a naturalist who wrote the organ of the species.

Q: Who was Benjamin Franklin?
A: Benjamin Franklin produced electricity by rubbing cats backwards.

Q: Name the four seasons.
A: Salt, pepper, mustard, and vinegar.

Q: Explain one of the processes by which water can be made safe to drink.
A: Flirtation makes water safe to drink because it removes large pollutants like grit, sand, dead sheep, and canoeists.

Q: What guarantees may a mortgage company insist on?
A: If you are buying a house, they will insist you are well endowed.

Q: What are steroids?
A: Things for keeping carpets still on the stairs.

Q: What happens to your body as you age?
A: When you get old, so do your bowels and you get intercontinental.

Q: What happens to a boy when he reaches puberty?
A: He says good-bye to his boyhood and looks forward to his adultery.

Q: Name a major disease associated with cigarettes.
A: Premature death.

Q: What is the Fibula?
A: A small lie.

Q: What does "varicose" mean?
A: Nearby.

Q: What is a seizure?
A: A Roman emperor.

Q: What is a terminal illness?
A: When you are sick at the airport.

Q: Use the word "judicious" in a sentence to show you understand its meaning.
A: Hands that judicious can be soft as your face.

Q: What does the word "benign" mean?
A: Benign is what you will be after you be eight.

Q: What is a turbine?
A: Something an Arab wears on his head.

Q: What is a Hindu?
A: It lay eggs.

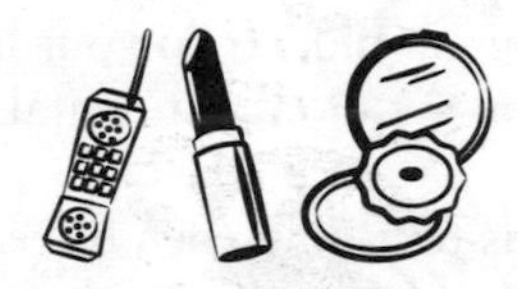

The Objects Inside Mum's Purse Or Handbag

A tissue smeared with make-up for dabbing children's faces as they go into school.

A shop loyalty card with more points than the British railway network.

A stash of money-off vouchers from every shop imaginable (every little helps).

A small packet of biscuits as emergency pacifiers when children are acting up in public places.

A supply of headache pills, pick-me-ups and assorted anxiety cures that could adequately stock a small chemist's shop.

A credit card whose lettering has almost been completely obliterated through overuse.

A small selection of stones, acorns, shells and other treasures your toddler has forced you to look after.

A mobile phone with teeth marks.

Plasters, inhalers, antiseptic cream and various other medical equipment that makes you feel like an emergency doctor permanently on call.

Messages Mums Don't Want To Receive While They're Out At Work

Dad saying he may be home "a bit late".

The school secretary phoning to say, "Nothing to worry about, but one of the kids has just bumped his/her head, and it may be best to whip them up to A & E immediately 'just to be on the safe side.'"

The babysitter cancelling at the last minute when you were just about to have your first night out in over four years.

The local police station phoning to ask, "Are you the mother of...?"

A garbled second hand message from an elderly neighbour saying they're not sure, but they think they just saw one of your children shoplifting in the High Street.

Another mum asking if you'd mind picking up their child as well and possibly laying on tea, too.

The next-door neighbour asking why your kids are having a party at three in the afternoon.

The local paper asking if you minded your child being photographed as the ring leader of a riot outside the school.

Mums And Teenagers

I hate you! You don't understand! I'm going to my room! Slamming doors, storming out, mysterious texts and trysts and ten years of schooling down the drain as your teenage offspring revert to the language of the caveman and a secrecy that would be the envy of the Knights Templar, the Freemasons and the French wartime resistance. Mum, how could you possibly understand? You've never been a teenager have you? Oh, you have? When was that then?

You know your children are growing up when they stop asking you where they came from and start refusing to tell you where they're going.

Adolescence is the age at which children stop asking questions because they know all the answers.

Definition of an adolescent: a new dog learning old tricks.

A young teenage girl comes home late one night and her mother asks her where she's been and who's she's been with. "I've just been out with a girl I know," she answers. "Are you sure you weren't out with a boy?" asks her mum. "Boy, girl, what's the difference?" asks the daughter, moodily. "Well," says Mum, "I suppose if you don't know the difference yet it doesn't really matter either way."

Late one Saturday night a woman is woken up by the phone ringing. Very grumpily she gets out of bed and goes to answer it. From the other end of the phone she hears a voice rushing breathlessly into a lengthy speech: "Hi, Mum, this is Susan. I'm really sorry I woke you up, but I had to call because I'm going to be a bit late getting home. I've somehow managed to get a flat tyre on your car. But it's not my fault. Honest! I don't know what happened. The tyre just went flat while we were inside the cinema. I'm really sorry, mum. Please don't be cross." Unfortunately Susan has misdialled and isn't on the phone to her mother. In fact the woman she's accidentally called doesn't have any daughters at all and tells her, "I'm sorry but I think you must have dialled the wrong number. I don't have a daughter named Susan." There's a pause and then the girl on the other end of the phone says, "Gosh, Mum, I knew you'd be cross but I didn't think you'd be that cross!"

A mum and a dad got their 16-year-old a gift of an expensive brand new mobile phone on condition that he would use it to phone home and let them know where he was if he was out late. One Saturday night the mum was waiting up for her son to come home and fell asleep in front of the television. A couple of hours later she woke up and realised there was no sign of him coming home and he hadn't bothered to call. The mum was furious. She snatched up the home and phone and punched in his number. When he answered, the mum demanded, "Where are you, and why haven't you bothered to call us like we arranged?" The boy replied rather sleepily, "But, mum, I'm upstairs in bed. I've been home for over an hour!"

"Watching your daughter being collected by her date feels like handing a million dollar Stradivarius over to a gorilla."

Jim Bishop

A teenage girl walks up to the assistant in a clothes shop. She hands over a dress she bought the day before and asks if she can exchange it. "What's wrong with it?" asks the assistant. "Too big, too small, wrong colour?" "No," says the teenager. "What's the problem with it then?" asks the assistant. "My mum thinks it looks great," replies the teenager.

Mum was frantic with worry. It was two o'clock in the morning and her seventeen-year-old daughter wasn't home from a night out with friends. She'd recently lost her mobile phone and so her mum couldn't call her, and she couldn't find all her friends" phone numbers because they were on her mobile too. Then she had a brainwave – she turned on her daughter's computer and emailed all her friends asking if anyone knew where she was. Almost straight away she received 23 replies from various friends all saying not to worry, her daughter was staying with them and had forgotten to phone.

"Definition of adolescence: A kind of emotional seasickness."

Arthur Koestler

Teenage is a moment that seems like an eternity; a time of perpetual emotion, cured by time, which brought it on in the first place.

Sixteen-year-old Shaun arrives home one day driving a Ferrari and his parents are astounded. "Where on Earth did you get that car?" his father demands. "It's OK," says Shaun. "I've just bought it." "Bought it? What with?" ask Mum and Dad. "With my own money," says Shaun. "What do you mean, 'your own money?'" asks his mother. "Since when have you had the money for a car like that?" "Stop worrying will you," says Shaun, "It only cost me twenty quid." And now his parents are absolutely amazed. "Twenty quid?! Who would sell a Ferrari to a boy of your age for 20 pounds?" asks dad. "It's all right," he says, "Nothing to worry about at all. It was Mrs Chapman three doors down. She saw me go past on my bike and asked me if I wanted to buy a Ferrari for 20 quid." "Oh, I get it now," says his mum, "Mrs Chapman's just the sort of older woman who'd love to get her hands on a young toy boy like you." "Absolutely disgusting," says Dad. "Let's all go and have a word with Mrs Chapman right now!" So they all troop round and find Mrs Chapman relaxing on her sun lounger in the garden. "What's going on, Mrs Chapman?" ask Mum and Dad. "Apparently you sold our son a Ferrari for 20 pounds." "Yes I did," says Mrs Chapman. "Last night my husband called. I thought he was up at his mother's in Northumberland, but it turns out he's run off to Hawaii with his secretary. After 25 years of marriage he says he's not coming back, and he asked me to sell his sports car and send him the money. So I did."

Mothers of teens know why some animals eat their young.

The hardest thing in the world is to raise children. Especially first thing in the morning, when they're teenagers.

A girl comes sobbing to her mother that she's pregnant. "Oh no! How could you?" yells the mum. "So come on! Who's the father?" "How would I know?" sniffs the girl. "You never let me go steady with anyone."

Raising a teenager is a bit like trying to nail some jelly to a tree.

Adolescence is the age when children try to bring up their parents.

I wish I could be just half as wonderful as my child thought I was when he was small. Or alternatively just half as stupid as my teenager now thinks I am.

> **"A boy becomes an adult three years before his parents think he does, and about two years after he thinks he does."**
>
> **General Lewis B. Hershey**

It rarely occurs to teenagers that the day will come when they'll know as little as their parents.

A high school teacher was talking to her class about surfing and asked if any of them knew when surfing was particularly popular in the USA: One of the girls in the class put up her hand and said, "The 60s!" "OK. Very good," said the teacher. "Can you be any more specific than that?" "Er," said the girl, "The 1960s?"

The first sign of maturity is the discovery that the volume knob also turns to the left.

Zoe brings her new boyfriend home to meet Mum, but Mum is completely horrified. Zoe's boyfriend is scruffy, has long straggly greasy hair, tattoos on his face and neck and piercings through his ears, nose and lips. When Zoe and her mum go to the kitchen to make some coffee, her mum turns to her and says, "I really don't think he's right for you, dear. He doesn't look very nice at all." "Oh Mum," replies Zoe, "You don't know him at all. You shouldn't judge people by their appearances. He's actually very public spirited." "Is he?" says mum. "Yes," says Zoe, "In fact at the moment he's doing 2,000 hours community service."

A mum is telling her friend how she manages to get her son out of bed in the morning. "It's not too difficult," she says, "I just open his door and toss the cat on his bed." "How does that get him out of bed?" asks the friend. "He sleeps with his dog," says the mum.

"Hey, Mum," asks teenager Johnny, "Can you give me 25 pounds?" "Certainly not," says mother. "OK," says Johnny, "I'll tell you what. If you give me the money, I'll tell you what dad said to the au pair when you were out at the beauty shop." His mother's ears perk up at this and she swiftly grabs her purse and hands over a wad of cash. "OK then," she says. "Now tell me what he said." "He said," says Johnny, "'Hey, Marie, make sure you wash my socks tomorrow.'"

Teenager Dave was walking down the high street one day when he was stopped by a charity collector. "Excuse me," said the woman, "Would you like to make a contribution to the old people's home?" "Certainly would," said Dave, "You can have my mum and dad."

Why is it that teenagers know everything apart from why they haven't tidied their rooms?

Susie has just got pregnant by her boyfriend at the age of 17 and after telling her father is sitting down being comforted by her mother. "So," says mum, "What did you father say when you told him you were pregnant?" "Do you want me to tell you exactly what he said or shall I leave out all the swear words?" Mum looks a bit shocked, "Yes please, dear. Leave out all the swear words." "Well in that case," says Susie, "He didn't really say anything at all."

A single mum is asked by a friend what her son is taking in college. She says with a sigh, "Everything I have."

Advice for teenagers:
If you really want to hurt your parents and you don't have enough nerve to be homosexual, the least you can do is study the arts at university.

> **"You have a wonderful child. Then, when he's 13, gremlins carry him away and leave in his place a stranger who gives you not a moment's peace... You have to hang in there, because two or three years later, the gremlins will return your child, and he will be wonderful again."**
>
> **Jill Eikenberg**

A boy who's recently gone to university phones his mother to let her know he's OK. "So how are you, Mum?" he asks. "Not too good son," she replies, "In fact I have eaten for 47 days." "You haven't eaten for 47 days?" he exclaims. "That's terrible. Why not, Mum?" "Because I didn't want to have my mouth full when you phoned."

Before we judge the younger generation, shouldn't we remember who brought them up?

A Teenager Is...

A person who can't remember to walk the dog but never forgets a phone number.

A weight watcher who goes on a diet by giving up candy bars before breakfast.

A youngster who receives his/her allowance on Monday, spends it on Tuesday, and borrows from his/her best friend on Wednesday.

Someone who can hear a favourite song played three streets away, but not his mother calling from the next room.

A whizz who can operate the latest computer without a lesson but can't make a bed.

A student who will spend 12 minutes studying for her history exam and 12 hours for her driver's license.

A youngster who is well informed about anything he doesn't have to study.

An enthusiast who has the energy to ride a bike for miles, but is usually too tired to dry the dishes.

A connoisseur of two kinds of fine music: Loud and Very Loud.

A young woman who loves the cat and tolerates her brother.

A person who is always late for dinner but always on time for a rock concert.

A romantic who never falls in love more than once a week.

A budding beauty who never smiles until her braces come off.

A boy who can sleep until noon on any Saturday when he suspects the lawn needs mowing.

An original thinker who is positive that her mother was never a teenager.

How To Spot The Mother Of A Teenager

Constantly texting as this is now sole means of communication with anyone under 20 (talking is like so uncool).

Jumping every time the phone rings in case it's the police, the hospital, or – you never know – the teenager themselves.

She's the one driving out of the garage at 2am to pick the teenager up from the pub, party or pavement.

All alcohol in house is under lock and key.

She can actually name new bands being played on radio courtesy of constant brainwashing.

She's wearing the latest fashion because she gets inside information.

Due to constant interaction with the teenager she's now become fluent in communicating in grunts.

Whenever she's out with her child you can see the teenager slouching along ten paces behind her.

Turning Teenager – Spotting The Signs

Instead of running up stairs they begin to stomp.

The bathroom is suddenly locked for what seems like days at a time.

Their bedroom is suddenly a no-go area for the rest of the family.

Their entire existence takes on a secretiveness that would make MI5 look like it was having an Open House day.

After years of steadily improving verbal skills they begin to communicate exclusively in Neanderthal grunts (this may be slightly modified when wanting to borrow money).

They have completely taken over the bathroom cabinet.

There is suddenly a whole bunch of other teenagers in your house at odd times of the day and night.

They completely stop eating at the table and instead wander around munching toast and whatever else they can scavenge.

The have lost the ability to stand upright.

They never sit on the sofa anymore they simply lie on it – even when they've only just got out of bed.

How Students Know When To Do Laundry

You're wearing your last pair of underwear in the shower consistently.

You've worn your sheets to school because you can't get them off of you.

Your socks feel like a shirt does when heavily starched, and they even smell through your trainers.

Your roommate walks around wearing a full body medical suit like the characters did in the movie *Outbreak* to avoid catching the Ebola virus.

The local police drug-sniffing dog is always coming by to sniff your laundry because of the strong stench.

Even after sewing 28 spring scented dryer sheets to the inside of your shirt, your friends still say you reek.

The phrase "Wash Me" is visibly written in your jeans.

Your red T-shirt is now green.

Excuses Mum Will Hear When Her Teenage Offspring Bring Back Their Laundry For Her To Do

Oh Mum! I've been missing you so much!

I didn't know what setting to use for Snakebite and Thai green curry stains.

Your washing always comes out better than mine, and I haven't got an iron yet either.

The laundrette's always full of weirdos.

I thought we could have a nice chat, and maybe a meal, while it's spinning round.

Can you believe it! There's just been another power cut at my place!

I've come to help you sort out your computer. Oh, and while I'm doing that can you bung this lot in the washing machine?

I kept throwing my dirty clothes on the floor in my flat but they didn't reappear clean and folded at the end of my bed like they used to at home.

Ten Signs Your Amish Teenager Is In Trouble

He sometimes stays in bed until after 5am.

In his sock drawer, you find pictures of women without bonnets.

He shows up at barn raisings in full "Kiss" makeup.

When you criticise him about anything, he yells, "Thou sucketh!"

Although his real name is Jebediah, he now he prefers to go by the name of "Jeb Daddy."

He defiantly tells you, "If I had a radio, I'd listen to rap."

You find his secret stash of coloured socks.

He uses slang expression such as: "Talk to the hand, 'cause the beard ain't listening."

He was recently pulled over for "driving his cart under the influence of cottage cheese."

He's taken to wearing his big black hat backwards.

More Of Mum's Best Jokes About Men

Q: What can you instantly tell about a well-dressed man?
A: His wife is good at choosing his clothes.

Q: What has eight arms and an IQ of 60?
A: Four men watching a football game.

Q: When does a man think about having a candlelight dinner?
A: When there's a power failure.

Q: What can you give a man who has everything?
A: A woman to show him how to work it.

Q: What's a man's definition of a romantic evening?
A: Sex.

Q: What's the difference between a new husband and a new dog?
A: A dog is always happy to see you and only takes a month to train.

Q: Why can't men catch mad cow disease?
A: Because they're all pigs.

Q: Why did God create man before he created woman?
A: You know you're always supposed to do a rough draft before you create your ultimate masterpiece.

Q: Why do female black widow spiders kill their males immediately after mating?
A: To stop the snoring before it starts.

Q: Why do men buy electric lawn mowers?
A: It helps them find their way back to the house.

Q: Why is it difficult to find men who are sensitive, caring and good looking?
A: These men already have boyfriends.

Q: Why do men carry on chasing women they have no intention of marrying?
A: For the same reason that dogs chase cars they have no intention of driving.

Q: Why do men like frozen microwave food so much?
A: That way they can do both the things they like in less than five minutes – eating and making love.

Q: Why do men like smart women?
A: Opposites attract.

Q: Why is psychoanalysis so much easier for men than it is for women?
A: When it's time to go back to childhood, he's already there.

Q: Why is sleeping with a man like a soap opera?
A: Just when you're beginning to get interested, they're finished until next time.

Q: What's the difference between a man and childbirth?
A: One is horrendously painful and involves lots of screaming, the other is just having a baby.

Q: How many men does it take to change a roll of toilet paper?
A: Nobody knows. It hasn't happened yet.

Q: Why do men get married?
A: So at last they can stop holding their stomachs in.

Q: Why don't men have mid-life crises?
A: No need – they just stay stuck in adolescence.

Q: Why are women called birds?
A: Because they like to pick up worms.

Q: What's the difference between men and women?
A: A woman wants one man to satisfy her every need. A man wants every woman to satisfy his one need.

Q: Why are there so many problems in men and women's relationships?
A: Women want a relationship without the complication of unnecessary sex, whereas men want sex without the complication of an unnecessary relationship.

Q: What do you call a man who's just had sex?
A: Anything you damn well like – he's fast asleep.

Q: What are the two reasons why men don't mind their own business?
A: One: no mind. Two: no business.

Incredible Mums Of The Natural World!

Over her lifetime a single female oyster can produce more than 100 million young. That must surely mean one heck of a lot of incoming phone calls every Mothers' Day, mustn't it?

A mother giraffe will often give birth standing up. This means a newborn giraffe's first experience will be a six foot drop. And the first words it hears will be its mother saying, "That's life, son! Get used to it!"

A kangaroo mother holds a reserve embryo inside after the first born baby has crawled up and out into her pouch. This embryo serves an "emergency back-up" child, should anything happen to the first. In moments of stress, try telling your kids you've adopted the same system.

Like human beings, mother chimpanzees will often develop lifelong relationships with their offspring. The difference is the baby chimpanzees usually keep their bedrooms tidier and have better table manners.

Tiger shark embryos will fight with each other while they're in their mother's womb. The baby shark that gets born is the winner. A fight to the death before you've even left the womb! Life really is tough for some, isn't it?

For at least the first six months of their lives, baby baleen whales depend entirely on their mother's milk diet. For the first 18 years of their lives, human offspring depend entirely on their mother's milk, cheese and other various items they find in her refrigerator.

Kittens are born both blind and deaf, but they can feel the vibration of their mother's purring which acts like a homing device so they can find their way to feed. We just shout, "Grub's up," but the kids still seem to blind and deaf when it's time to help with the washing up.

When baby opossum are born, they are so small that an entire litter can fit in a tablespoon. They live inside their mother's pouch for three months before climbing out and riding on her back. So good presents to buy for young opossum mothers include tablespoons instead of prams or playpens for when the kids are little and then, after three months, a series of appointments with a back specialist.

If frightened or threatened, a mother rabbit may abandon, ignore or eat her young. So just tell your kids, "Whatever you do, children, don't say 'Boo' or I might accidentally eat you."

Advice From Kids On Romantic Issues

"Love will find you, even if you are trying to hide from it. I've been trying to hide from it since I was five, but the girls keep finding me."

Boy aged eight

"Romantic adults usually are all dressed up, so if they are just wearing jeans it might mean they used to go out or they just broke up."

Girl aged nine (on dating)

"They want to make sure their rings don't fall off, because they paid good money for them."

Boy aged eight (on why people in love with each other hold hands)

Cats And Kiddens

Some people, they say, have pets as substitute kids. But what about the ways in which kids are like substitute pets? Cats start off as helpless and loveable little kittens that you adore and indulge – then they turn into cats. A bit like kids turning into teenagers.

Kids/kittens jump playfully all over the sofa and get off when you tell them, but teenagers/cats suddenly hog the sofa all to themselves and you end up having to sit somewhere else.

Kids/kittens have to be given milk and sloppy food that's easy to eat, then when they become teenagers/cats they turn their noses up at what you put in front of them and grab some grub when they're out on the town.

Kids/kittens come and let you know when they want to play, teenagers/cats just disappear and have a good time who knows where and roll in at any hour they damn well choose.

Kids/kittens make a mess but they can't help it so you forgive them, teenagers/cats become fastidious about their personal grooming but still can't help leaving clumps of hair and greasy marks all over the furniture.

Kids/kittens sleep at odd times of the day and then suddenly come alive and want to play just when you want to relax; teenagers/cats sleep half the day then roam the streets in the hours of darkness.

Kids/kittens keep you amused for hours with their funny antics, teenagers/cats suddenly become very solemn and aloof and look at you disdainfully if you find something they've done amusing.

Kids/kittens will follow you round the house and get under your feet, teenagers/cats disappear for hours on end and then are suddenly noticed curled up asleep as if they've never been away.

You're A Stressed Mum If...

- You take dinner out of the oven only to find that it hadn't actually been switched on.
- You're shouting and swearing at other road users even when you're just pushing a baby buggy.

- You're using the baby's dummy to try and calm yourself down.
- You not only have to write lists to remember everything, you also have "remember to write list" scrawled on the kitchen notice board.
- You queue outside a curiously quiet school gate only to remember that it's the summer holidays and the kids are at the park with Dad.
- You're found sleepwalking with a buggy.
- You're ready for bed before the kids are.
- You want to see the doctor for tranquillizers but can't find time to get there.

All You Need To Know About Mothers As Told By Primary School Children

What does your mum do in her spare time?

Mothers don't do spare time.
According to her, she pays bills all day long.

What would it take to make your mum perfect?

On the inside she's already perfect. Outside, I think some kind of plastic surgery.
Diet. You know, her hair. I'd diet, maybe blue.

Describe the world's greatest mum?

She would make broccoli taste like ice cream!
The greatest mum in the world wouldn't make me kiss my fat aunts!
She'd always be smiling and keep her opinions to herself.

If you could change one thing about your mum, what would it be?

She has this weird thing about me keeping my room clean. I'd get rid of that.
I'd make my mum smarter. Then she would know it was my sister who did it and not me.

Is anything about your mum perfect?

Her teeth are perfect, but she bought them from the dentist.
Her casserole recipes. But we hate them.
Just her children.

Letter to Mum

I entered my daughter's bedroom and saw a letter over the bed. With the worst premonition, I read it with trembling hands...

Dear Mum,

It is with great regret and sorrow that I'm telling you I eloped with my new boyfriend.

I have found real passion and he is so nice, with all his piercings and tattoos and his big motorbike.

But it's not only that Mum, I'm pregnant and Ahmed said that we will be very happy in his caravan in the woods. He wants to have many more children with me and that's one of my dreams too.

Don't worry Mum, I'm 15 years old now and I know how to take care of myself. Some day I'll visit so you can get to know your grandchildren.

Love Jenna xxx

PS: Mum, it's not really true! I'm round next door. I just wanted to show you that there are worse things in life than my school report which is in my desk drawer... I love you!!!

Mums And Older Kids

They've finally flown the coop, and now you don't know what to do with yourself. Even worse, you could now have become that dreaded figure that has been the butt of bad jokes for centuries: the mother-in-law, which, as you may have been told elsewhere, is an anagram of Woman Hitler (no, really.) Ouch! And even if you're not a mother-in-law, you're in a strange netherworld like a lost soul in purgatory. You're neither a mother nor a free woman. You still worry about them, you still yearn to offer them advice when you see them making a complete hash of their lives on their own, but you have to keep your distance. But then occasionally, out of a clear blue sky one of your long-lost children will turn up on the doorstep all smiles and hugs just like the good old days – yes, precisely, they want their washing done. And, if anything just happens to be cooking...

On the set of one of his movies, Hollywood actor David Arquette found a collection of vintage editions of *Playboy* magazine. Unfortunately when he looked through one of them he found an image that he wished he hadn't: a picture of his mum playing table tennis at a nudist camp.

Three Jewish mothers, Nadine, Joyce, and Sylvia, are sitting on a park bench, talking about their children. Sylvia says, "Well friends, I have good news and bad news." Nadine says, "Oh yeah?" "Oh yes," says Sylvia. "My son Michael called me up on the phone last night and told me he was gay." "Oh no, Sylvia," says Joyce. "And after all you did for him! You were such a wonderful mother. Don't blame yourself." "Of course she was wonderful!" says Nadine. "But if that's the bad news, let's hear the good news?" "Well," says Sylvia, "The good news is he's marrying a doctor!"

"Human beings are the only creatures on earth that allow their children to come back home."

Bill Cosby

"People should know, that when they look at Eminem and think what a cool, tough guy he is, they should remember that he actually lived at home – with his mom – until he was 26."

Debbie Mathers (Eminem's mum)

"No matter how old a mother is, she watches her middle-aged children for signs of improvement."

Florida Scott-Maxwell

"Sometimes when I look at all my children, I say to myself, 'Lillian, you should have stayed a virgin.'"

Lillian Carter, at the 1980 Democratic Convention, at which her son Jimmy was nominated to run for a second term as US President (he didn't win!)

"I want my children to have all the things I couldn't afford. Then I want to move in with them."

Phyllis Diller

"I blame my mother for my poor sex life. All she told me was 'the man goes on top and the woman underneath.' For three years my husband and I slept in bunk beds."

Joan Rivers

A young man turns up in an excited state at his mother's house. "I've fallen in love and I want to get married," he tells her. "OK," says his mother, 'So when do I get to meet her?" "I've invited her over this afternoon," says the man. "She's coming over with a couple of her girlfriends. Hey! I've got an idea! Instead of me introducing her, why don't you see if you can guess which of the three girls is the one I want to marry?" So a bit later that day there's a knock at the door and the young man ushers in three beautiful young women, a blonde, a brunette and a redhead. He sits the three of them down on the sofa and says to his mother, "OK. Here they are. Now see if you can tell which of these fabulous women I'm going to marry." His mother looks them over a few times and says, "It's her! It's the redhead in the middle!" The young man and the redhead are delighted. "Wow! That's incredible," they say. "You've has picked the right one straight away. How on earth could you possibly tell?" And mother walks over and whispers in her son's ear, "I don't like her."

Is there anything more embarrassing than having to sit through a sexually explicit scene in a TV programme or a film in the presence of your mother? When he was making the film *When Harry Met Sally*, Rob Reiner had to demonstrate the mind blowing orgasm he wanted Meg Ryan to fake while she's sitting in a diner with Billy Crystal. The punch-line to the scene is of course the old lady at the next table who watches the whole performance and then says, "I'll have what she's having." Not only did Rob Reiner have to act out all the pounding, thumping and screaming of the orgasm in front of this old lady, the old lady was in fact his mother, Mrs Estelle Reiner.

Joe has just met his first serious girlfriend and is desperate to impress her. Naturally, he asks his mum's advice. She suggests persuading his flatmates to go out for the evening, then invite her round for a romantic candlelit dinner. "That's a great idea Mum, thanks," says Joe. The following week Joe's mum asked how it went. "Hmm, not too good I don't think mum." "Why not?" asks Mum. "Well, it was really embarrassing; she insisted on washing the plates." "So? What's wrong with that?" asks Mum. "It was before we'd put the food on them," said Joe.

A young Jewish man moved to the city to live in a studio apartment. Before he left, his mother gave him two dress shirts as a going away gift. One was blue and one was cream coloured. His mother was very nervous and wouldn't stop calling him to ask him to move back home from the "ghetto". The young man invited his mum over to dinner the next week in order to show her that the neighbourhood was safe. She arrived on time with Dad and a shopping bag full of food because she knew he was bound to be starving. When he opened the door his mum frowned. The young man was worried and asked, "Mum, what's wrong?" She replied, "What's the matter, you didn't like the other shirt?"

Coming to terms with all the bad points about your character is a good first step to the next stage of self-improvement – blaming your mum and dad.

Groucho Marx was staying at a hotel in Italy. One day he was in the hotel lift when it stopped at a floor and a group of priests got in. One of the priests recognised Groucho and told him, "My mother is a great fan of yours." "Wow!" said Groucho. "I didn't know you guys were allowed to have mothers."

A mum is moaning to her friend about her hopeless son, "He's never managed to hold down a job in his life. The only time he made any money for himself was when his baby teeth came out."

A man is walking through Las Vegas one night when a woman approaches him and tells him that for 25 dollars she will give him a darn good spanking. When he gets back to his hotel room he immediately phones his mother and says, "Mum, you should come over. You could make an awful lot of money round here."

Franklin D Roosevelt, US President from 1933 to 1945, recalled that he had never in his entire life walked out of his mother's house without hearing her call after him: "Franklin! Are you sure you're dressed warmly enough?"

"Sometimes I feel older than my mum."

Britney Spears

"Graduation day is tough for adults. They go to the ceremony as parents. They come home as contemporaries. After 22 years of child-rearing, they are unemployed."

Erma Bombeck

"The first half of our life is ruined by our parents and the second half by our children."

Clarence Darrow

"You see much more of your children once they leave home."

Lucille Ball

"Always be nice to your children because they are the ones who will choose your rest home."

Phyllis Diller

"When mothers talk about the depression of the empty nest, they're not mourning the passing of all those wet towels on the floor, or the music that numbs your teeth, or even the bottle of capless shampoo dribbling down the shower drain. They're upset because they've gone from supervisor of a child's life to a spectator. It's like being the vice president of the United States."

Erma Bombeck

Jim has had trouble finding a girlfriend that his mum will approve of for years, so he asks the advice of the wife of one of his friends. "What you need to do," she says, "Is find a woman who's like your mum, then she's bound to approve." Jim is so desperate to find a girlfriend that his mum will be happy with that he agrees, and sets off on a quest to find a girl just like her. After going through several dating agencies he finds just the girl. She's uncannily similar to his mum when she was younger. She looks like her, dresses like her, has her hair like her and even has similar interests. He's so pleased he immediately takes her home to meet his parents. "So," says his friend's wife the next day, "Did your mum approve of her?" "Yes," said Jim, "She approved all right, but my dad hated her guts."

> **"Years ago, my mother gave me a bullet, and I put it in my breast pocket. Two years after that, I was walking down the street, when a berserk Evangelist heaved a bible out of a hotel room window, hitting me in the chest. The bible would have gone through my heart if it wasn't for that bullet."**
>
> **Woody Allen**

A daughter breaks up with her boyfriend and asks her mum for advice about returning the many gifts he's given her. Without a pause, her mum tells her, "Send back the stuffed animals and the letters, but tell him you're keeping the jewellery for sentimental reasons."

Princess Anne is opening a new library in the little town of Chipping Sodbury. When she arrives there she is wearing a rather ostentatious red fur hat. As she's introduced to the head librarian he comments on her unusual choice of headgear. "It was Mummy's idea actually," she replies, "When I told her last night I was going to Chipping Sodbury today she immediately said 'Chipping Sodbury? Wear the fox hat?'"

Hollywood movie director and former *Happy Days* star Ron Howard won the Academy Award for Best Director in 2000 for his film *A Beautiful Mind*. He said in his acceptance speech, "I'm not a good enough actor any more to stand up here and make you believe that I haven't imagined this moment and played it out a thousand times over the years... Before my mom passed away about 18 months ago, she predicted that this would happen for me on this film. But she also predicted that this would happen for every film I've made since 1983."

> **"I'm in Bolton, so I won't have to give me mum three rings to let her know I'm home safe. Do you do that? Give her three rings. And after the second ring she picks it up. What's the point of that?"**
>
> **Peter Kay**

Leigh Walker, goalie for Conference league side Scarborough FC was chuffed to find his team up against Premiership team Chelsea in the FA Cup in January 2004. Walker played the game of his life against Chelsea, and as a memento of the event his opposite number in the game, Chelsea goalkeeper Carlo Cudicini, handed him his Chelsea shirt, which he had autographed specially. This would have been great, and something that Leigh would have treasured for the rest of his life, but unfortunately after he took the shirt home his mum found it, thought it looked a bit dirty and decided to give it a good clean in the washing machine.

Children despise their parents up until the age of 40, when they suddenly become just like them, thus preserving the system.

> **"Whenever I fill out a job application, for the part that says, 'In Case Of Emergency Notify:', I put 'Doctor'. What's my mother going to do? 'Okay, I'm here. Open him up.'"**
>
> **Steven Wright**

Christmas Letter From A Mum

Dear Darling Son and That Person You Married,

Merry Christmas to you, and please don't worry. I'm just fine considering I can't breathe or eat. The important thing is that you have a nice holiday, thousands of miles away from your ailing mother. I've sent along my last ten pounds in this card, which I hope you'll spend on my grandchildren. God knows their mother never buys them anything nice. They look so thin in their pictures, poor babies.

Thank you so much for the Christmas flowers, dear boy. I put them in the freezer so they'll stay fresh for my grave. Which reminds me – we buried Grandma last week. I know she died years ago, but I got to yearning for a good funeral so Aunt Viola and I dug her up and had the service all over again. I would have invited you, but I know that woman you live with would have never let you come. I bet she's never even watched that videotape of my haemorrhoid surgery, has she?

Well son, it's time for me to crawl off to bed now. I lost my cane beating off muggers last week, but don't you worry about me. I'm also getting used to the cold since they turned my heat off and am grateful because the frost on my bed numbs the constant pain. Now don't you even think about sending any more money, because I know you need it for those expensive family vacations you take every year. Give my love to my darling grandbabies and my regards to whatever-her-name-is – the one with the black roots who stole you screaming from my bosom.

Merry Christmas.

Love, Mum